PRAISE FOR
A NEW WAY TO WEALTH

"*A New Way to Wealth* is a master work on work in a world of change. Piasecki has done it again—33 years after being one of the first to write about climate change and the search for environmental excellence."

—Chris Coulter
CEO, GlobeScan

"Inspired by the way Bob Dylan, Bruce Springsteen, and Ben Franklin lived their creative lives, *A New Way to Wealth* is the catalyst needed for a conversation that you, your company, or your industry use now to open up a pathway to discover your own solutions."

—Bobby Carlton
Director of Immersive Learning, Ready Learner One

"After a lifetime of experience in business and government, Piasecki is calling for a new era of restraint, frugality, and public-mindedness—not as PR window dressing, but as a set of non-negotiable first principles."

—Daniel Sherrell
Author of Warmth: Coming of Age
at the End of Our World

"Piasecki has created a new metric in these pages, the concept of 'competitive frugality,' explained in practical detail as a way of developing social capital and spending it in a respectful way. In doing this, Piasecki helps on climate change, personal self-actualization, and corporate competition in one coherent swoop."

—Richard Ellis
*Vice President, Corporate Social Responsibility,
Walgreens Boots Alliance*

"Piasecki provides a message for our carbon- and capital-constrained world. Clever and informed, his nineteenth book delivers an urgent, articulate call for a future that is at once frugal and fulfilling, and, most importantly, sustainable."

—Paul Grondahl
Director of the NYS Writers Institute at
the University at Albany, and author of several books

"In a world increasingly constrained by planetary boundaries and the impacts of climate and social change, this book is both intelligent and fun. It brings together the full extent of Bruce's personal experience and journey—along with the unique individuals with whom he has worked over decades—to offer wonderful insights on what it takes to transform to a purposeful, sustainable, and winning enterprise."

—Dr. Dominic Emery
Chief of Staff, bp

"Institutions—be they private, public, academic, or others—can be agents for positive change. Those organizations that 'get it' will continue to endure, evolve, and succeed. *A New Way to Wealth* can be a source of inspiration and sustainable success for organizations that 'get it.'"

—Brian Kellogg
Director, Global EHS, KLA

"Bruce Piasecki's latest book reminds us of the importance of the traditional principles of personal integrity, frugality, and a genuine concern for others. For anyone who seeks to lead today, understanding these principles and learning how to apply them effectively are essential, and Piasecki's latest book will help you do that."

—Ken Strassner
Yale Attorney

"*A New Way to Wealth* calls us away from the mindless dribble of competition for merely personal gain, to commit to business and personal practices that sustain and bring wealth to the common good as well. A book to buy, read remember, and cherish."

—L. Rostaing (Ross) Tharaud
Attorney

"Bruce Piasecki's newest book colorfully describes the secret to organizational success in the age of climate change—competitive frugality! Not mere belt-tightening, but the joyful pursuit of innovations that efficiently build social capital. Piasecki is a man of insight and heart; we would do well to follow his lead."

—William Throop
Professor Emeritus of Philosophy and Environmental Studies, Green Mountain College

"Piasecki describes 'a world riddled by surveillance capitalism, rampant consumerism, and power politics,' where every decision/preference/thought become commodities. In this compelling book after his fantastic *2040: A Fable*, Bruce Piasecki offers the notion of doing more with less. We need to embrace a concept of competitive frontiers informed by planetary boundaries, and find solutions that address business value, social needs and environmental health. His words give us hope and direction."

—Dinah A. Koehler, Sc.D.
Harvard, Board Member of the Medical Consortium on Climate and Public Health

A SELECTION OF OTHER BOOKS
BY BRUCE PIASECKI

Doing More With Teams

World Inc
(in English and foreign editions)

Corporate Environmental Strategy

Diplomacy and Longevity:
The Lives of Frank Loy and Steve Percy

Environmental Management
and Business Strategy

Giants of Social Investing:
John Streur and Jack Robinson

Swallowing the Earth Whole:
The Lives of Frank Loy and Steve Percy

Doing More With Less

In Search of Environmental Excellence

Missing Persons: A Memoir

New World Companies

The Quiet Genius of Eileen Fisher

The Social Intelligence of Linda Coady

The Surprising Solution
(Updated paperback edition of *World Inc*)

A *New* Way TO Wealth

The Power of
Doing More
with Less

Bruce Piasecki

A *New* Way to Wealth

The Power of Doing More with Less

by Bruce Piasecki

Ordering Information for Print Editions

Quantity Sales: Contact awards@ahcgroup.com for discounted bulk
orders over 10 units of any title by Bruce Piasecki, including prior
books. These rates go as high as a 50 percent discount for orders
over 50 books; and the rate is dependent on the email request and
intended use. Expect between 20 and 50 percent off list price.

Orders for Board or College Use: The founder of the Creative Force
Foundation, Inc, in seeking broad use of these books for Boards
of Directors and the new generation of business and society users,
offers an across-the-board discount of 30 percent for Board and
School uses. Orders should be directed to awards@ahcgroup.com.

ISBN: 978-1-66781-912-9

Printed and distributed by BookBaby
(www.bookbaby.com)

Printed in the United State of America

10 9 8 7 6 5 4 3 2 1

Deep, lasting thanks for the book inputs
from Peter Lynch,
Amin Mohamed,
and Tom Bonaccio.

In addition, deep thanks for the
design and compositional support
from Debbi Wraga
and Frank Weaver.

TABLE OF CONTENTS

INTRODUCTION

By Micah Shippee, Ph.D.,
CEO, Ready Learner One

A New Way to Wealth is Bruce Piasecki's nineteenth book.

This short but smart new book is based on his 40 years as the owner and CEO of a management consulting firm that knows firsthand the power of doing more with less. Piasecki's firm, AHC Group (www.ahcgroup.com), has helped Toyota enter the global market with their hybrid powertrain. They helped Walmart enter Africa efficiently, with strategic partners across five years. In recent years, they worked on competitive frugality with such globe-spanning giants as bp on its energy transformation, and Merck and Walgreens on their needs to flourish in a time of Covid-19.

Piasecki's career is about the art of competitive frugality. He grew up a factory kid on Long Island, made his way to Cornell as a basketball star, and up the corporate stairwells of the firms noted in his client history and an ongoing series of biannual membership workshops known as the Corporate Affiliates Workshops.

What you are about to experience is the ultimate summary of his career: a down-to-earth, readable, and optimistic narrative in nine chapters and a prelude that sing.

THE NATURE OF MODERN WORK

To study Piasecki's work is to study the changing nature of work itself, and to reflect on how the best firms compete and thrive. Piasecki builds himself on the shoulders of other giants like Jim Collins, and Harvard's business gurus, as well as on the shoulders of the six leaders he has written biographies about. But what matters is his insight into what will help us in life, careers, families, and friends.

The nature of modern work is changing because the world is changing. Insights into the future of work largely explore our processes and workflows as they are related to modern technologies that are evolving and increasingly disruptive. In effect, we might be pressured to think of the future of work as doing more with more. However, our globalized society needs us to take more care and understand disruption and innovation in this time of carbon and capital constraints.

We are, after all, global citizens, humankind, children of one earth. Piasecki's new book is a just-in-time perspective challenging our status quo. He offers an intelligent guide for a successful future, while acknowledging what makes this a swift and severe new world.

HOW I WORK WITH DR. PIASECKI

I met Dr. Bruce Piasecki in a phone call through our mutual colleague, Bobby Carlton, the Executive Director of Immersive Experiences at Ready Learner One. His love of historical precedent and well-read nature are clear in his writings and conversation. We met over the next few months, via video-chat, to discuss Piasecki's work and aspiring legacy. As we entered a formal partnership, my firm began creating engaging course experiences leveraging the vast knowledgebase of Bruce's work.

As the CEO of a training and learning company, Ready Learner One, our collaborations focused on designing and developing courses around the themes of his books. As a result, the DOING MORE WITH LESS course delivers on its efforts to empower change agents to up-skill and find success. My field of study, instructional design, broadens out to not only include adult learning theory, but also organizational behavior and planned change. Like Bruce, I have worked in spaces and places to help people manage change.

In this book we will find guidance on just how to step back and capture, with grace and force, our competitive nature. Failure awaits those that cannot harness the skill of knowing how to "step back," and discover why doing more with less is success. Thus emerges a critical lens by which we must approach a world ready for change.

Fundamental to understanding the change process is understanding communication channels—that is, the what, when, why, and how of people communicating. This book explores the power of relationships and meaningful work in vivid detail and through lasting concepts.

We have learned over decades of research and analysis how the organizations/communities in which we communicate can accelerate or impede progress. While innovations create new and faster means of transmitting messages, the sender and receiver remain the interpreter of the motivation and meaning of the message. The relationship between the two is paramount in the effectiveness of the communication, and from this we have come to understand that positive relationships are the key to success. With this in mind, Piasecki's teams have worked diligently to accelerate progress with global organizations like Merck, bp, Walgreens, and others noted at www.ahcgroup.com. These experiences are captured in this book, an exploration into the two-way dialogue between social needs and business results. We can see this dance of dialogue, and its social value, throughout Piasecki's book. In fact, Gene Miller read some of his work as a "sustained conversation" of force and wit.

Piasecki's new book guides us in building our competitive nature as global citizens. Our communication has become more digital and less tangible, exposing a need for strong bonds of relationship. In a changing world, one truth remains: the power of relationships. Piasecki's practice is based on teams, and key relationships feed all of his books. In this power rests the ability to live a fulfilling life, to promote social good, and to achieve organizational growth. As one who practices what he preaches, Piasecki finds delight in collaborating with award-winning designer, innovator, and educator Bruce Mau (Massive Change Network). This collaboration is a testament to the power of leveraging relationships to amplify efforts and make the world a better place through thoughtful design and practical change. Piasecki brought Gordon Lambert, Bruce Mau, and Bill Novelli into his team serving bp, a 100-billion-dollar giant of immense complexity and need.

A master of networking, Piasecki has seen his efforts bonded with the legendary work of William Novelli (*Good Business: The Talk, Fight and Win Way to Change the World*). Novelli and Piasecki found themselves on the Board of Directors of the Medical Consortium on Climate and Public Health, sitting with a set of renowned doctors. In these connections and many more, we see the life experiences that led to this book.

FITTING PIASECKI INTO CULTURAL HISTORY

Dr. Piasecki's work is built on the historical shoulders of Ben Franklin and Abe Lincoln, amplified by titans of industry like Gene Miller (Gaining Ground), Chris Coulter (CEO of GlobeScan), and Patricia Aburdene (*New York Times* bestseller and co-author of the Megatrends series)—each of whom have written powerful introductions to Bruce Piasecki's prior books. These prior dozen plus books have solidified his work in the critical fields of corporate governance, energy, product, and environmental strategy.

In this new book, you will learn to:

- Explore your role as a leader in our changing society. Piasecki's approach helps you refine your skills at being frugal, inventive, and diplomatic.

- Navigate times when intervention is required to make massive changes in your life or firms. This helps you develop the competitive skills to be rapidly on-boarded in complex teams.

- Leverage your leadership skills to use social capital to create a culture of frugality during tough economic times.

As I reread this book, Piasecki helped me realize that the future importance of competition and frugality will mount with time; billions of people in this world will demand it.

WHAT DOES PIASECKI MEAN BY "COMPETITIVE FRUGALITY"?

There is a deep paradox and insight behind Piasecki's chapters. The word "frugality" speaks of self-restraint and self-control, two words not commonly found in business. Competitive Frugality is, after all, self-control employed to relinquish self-centeredness in order to stop wasting time, energy, and resources. This is the lasting gift in Piasecki's book.

In *A New Way to Wealth* we see how we must reframe our thinking to understand that opportunity abounds from the realignment of money, people, and rules.

Clearly, mega-companies have mega-responsibilities, yet they do not all embrace this fact, leading to their catastrophic downfall. Therein lies a competitive advantage—an intelligent form of competition—to see the needs of a heavily populated planet 5, 10, and 20 years down the road.

I consider myself well read in fields related to earning my doctorate, and to launching my firm, and I have found this book reveals new grounds for a hopeful future, as it cements classical competitive habits into our behaviors.

Today's smaller world requires frugality from governments, corporations, privately held firms, and individual homes. Piasecki advises us:

- The age of the consumer is giving way to a more creative age of restraint.

- We must burn off our self-centeredness and stop wasting time, energy, and resources.

- We need to find our competitive advantage through a more frugal path.

A New Way to Wealth will guide employees, learners, leaders, and organizations to be successful through frugality, to refocus with a sense of social purpose in capitalism, and to refine instincts for innovation and survival.

Enjoy your journey into this book!

Your guide, Dr. Bruce Piasecki, will expertly lead you through the knowledge acquisition necessary for you to bring positive change into your context. I hope you enjoy the parallel *immersive* learning experiences we are bringing to this work through Ready Learner One.

As I have found in my months with Bruce Piasecki, I have no doubt you will find introspective growth and the motivation to achieve success here.

—Micah Shippee Ph.D., CEO, Ready Learner One

Postscript by Author

I am deeply thankful for Dr. Shippee's generous introduction, as he connects the dots of my life work of management practice with the principles and the perspectives shared in this summary book.

I know how hard it is to write such a broad yet focused introduction. Reading Shippee's introduction here is like rewatching my favorite films: in a short period of time a range of emotions are described, and you leave the theater with eyes opened. Thank you, Dr. Shippee.

Author's Note:
A Vision to Embrace

This new book, my nineteenth in four decades of professional writing, derives from a comment from the late great American writer Tom Wolfe. In inviting me to join the Lotos Club in Manhattan, Tom Wolfe noted, "Your book about doing more with less (2012) can be re-made by you and your experiences in management and self-determination for the rest of the century."

He returned to that message annually for me with his hand-done, and witty, Christmas cards. I found that both supportive and something that gave me anxiety this last decade. For over ten years I read other books, and watched thousands of movies with my wife, to avoid this stimulating request by the late great author of the farce on banking and racism, *The Bonfire of the Vanities*.

Tom, like Jay Parini, knew there is an element of sportive seriousness in all I do, both at work as a change agent for complex firms and as a social historian when I write.

What follows attempts to honor that visionary Tom Wolfe comment. I hope you enjoy it.

—*Bruce Piasecki*

CHAPTER 1

⟳⟲

PRELUDE: SOME PRINCIPLES, AND A PROMISE

"So much for industry, my friends, and attention to one's own business; but to these we must add frugality, if we would make our industry more certainly successful."

—Ben Franklin, *The Way to Wealth*

• •

HOMAGE TO BEN FRANKLIN

Photo courtesy of: Jupiter Images | photos.com

This book is my homage to Benjamin Franklin. As I travel this world, I find people know Franklin as a great man, not just a great American. He has become, over 300 years, the first world citizen. For me, he represents the wisdom and wit of the past that is ever present.

By age 41, Franklin felt that he had spent enough time making money. Unlike most in business or the halls of power in governments, Franklin knew how to ask: "What is Enough?" And he knew when to realign his focus on money, people, and rules; so he devoted the second half of his life to making better products, better organizations. Ben became Big Ben as he wrote over decades a set of guidewords for promising people that enhanced society. In the pages that follow, you will see how he converted—how he transmuted, really—ordinary capitalist capital into social capital, the trick that remains at the crux of fixing the climate crisis we all now face.

The people of our new, modern world admire Franklin's **persistent prominence**. Nowadays, as I travel globally to mega cities, a taxi driver will often respond to the name Franklin with informed joy. I have been observing this global phenomenon about "American-born" inventive pragmatism since my *World Inc* book was translated into many different languages, including Greek, Portuguese, and Korean, and winning a book-of-the-year award in business in Japanese. Often as I engaged with a new culture, it was Franklin over whom we first shared bread and commonality.

While I am no Big Ben, I did stand on his shoulders in a sense, remaining pragmatic in business and government, while leaving a verbal record for my century. Franklin is the man at the birth of modernity, the man who understood that being industrious and frugal made us of this world. This is what organizes and blends the power in our principles.[1]

---

1   In conclusion, we should be shocked how Walter Isaacson's excellent new biography undervalues these points about frugality in Franklin. What will the new age think of Franklin, if they only learn about his politics, his love of the technical, and his horse-trading? Even the BBC specials on Franklin ignore his lasting insights into frugality!

The crux is consistent; by paying this homage to Franklin in style and deed, we are reminding ourselves of that primal first self that knew about fair competition and frugality.

I can see another value in beginning again with striving along the routes of Ben Franklin. His principles help us do what we refer to today as "self-actualization." This is very different from selfish "wellness" movements, where all the value is on the calm and confidences of the "me and the me generation." I know too many people we find extremely selfish in their needs for wellness.

Self-actualization, in this classic Ben Franklin sense, is about giving back, about stepping back to liberate more social capital in your friends, family, and firms. It is the essence of the positive side of corporate globalization (which we all know can be vicious and severe), and it is what enables the productive competitive self to work in more productive and impactful teams.

This book is not about simple ego liberation; it is about finding your route to being a giver, a person of impact in society.

What Do I Mean by Wealth?

During the months I was awarding Daniel Sherrell, age 31, my public charity's first annual writer's award, I thought a good deal about his generation and his brilliant concerns in *Warmth: Coming of Age at the End of Our World* (Penguin Books, 2021). When I first watched his Ted Talk, he conveyed in an eloquent 13 minutes the weight of being born into this century dominated by responses to climate change. Throughout our early talks, he asked me, "What do you mean by wealth?"—almost each time we exchanged ideas about the value in his campaign work and in his book.

For me, wealth includes the full glory of wealth creation, not just material gains. The things that have fulfilled me on my journey to wealth are the bonds at work and home, balanced with the joys of being in society. We explore here the entire role you play in fixing society's many woes—from family and friends to your firm and the world at large. This is your true wealth.

There is much to learn from the famous Ben Franklin. I learned this in teaching his *Autobiography* to undergraduates for nine years in the beginning of my career, and I never forgot how the Franklin mode of pragmatism rewired me. You must become like Ben Franklin all over again: frugal, inventive, and diplomatic. Once you learn to participate in this new larger wealth, the world becomes more intelligible, more acceptable.

Think of this book, then, as a learning tool—as a leisurely conversation with the most aspiring side of who you are. **Its goal is to help you unearth your competitive advantages on your way to wealth.**

You will meet many friends, clients, and CEOs in this book who will draw out your abilities to think in a frugal, diplomatic, and competitive way, where doing more with less is success. In my experience, friends start this widening experience.

Faith in Our Future

By the final chapters, you will have absorbed what I offer as new grounds for hope in a world riddled by surveillance capitalism, rampant consumerism, and power politics.

When I look over the books, friends, and clients that helped shape my life, I must acknowledge how they also helped develop my faith in the future.

Take again Daniel Sherrell. I found his book *Warmth* uplifting, even though it was centered on the dread of climate change. He will become for his generation a voice of "proto-optimism" and action. There are grounds for hope in the work found in this new generation and their labors. This tonal shift makes Sherrell's book so different from the endless stream of apocalyptic warnings at the center of many shelves since the 1970s. I will not bore you with these worrisome obstacles to your ascent, as you can contemplate them in the fable that I wrote during Covid-19 titled *2040*. The point is: cultivate through reading your faith in the future.

From sports and competition in business, I am painfully aware of the falsely competitive knuckleheads in our world. Think here about the "great" fallen cyclist Lance Armstrong, explored in my book on *Doing More With Teams*. Or think about the recent coverage on the fall of the Governor of New York State, Andrew Cuomo. Once you become a bully in your competitiveness, there will be no one there to pick you up. Yet we can think "past" these sets of self-imploding obstacles, and steer clear.

Where Do I Derive This Faith in the Future?

Much of the second half of this book is about **deriving a sense of faith in the future**. You cannot talk intelligently about faith until you spend six chapters on the fundamental higher facts of the present. There is too much climate anxiety and dismal politicizing of the future for my taste and your health. So let this book exfoliate before you. Yes, there is a re-current mantra, an over-arching undertow of faith and hope in the book.

Photo courtesy of: Tomasz Trojanowski | Shutterstock

You can call me a "despairing optimist"—to borrow a phrase coined in the 1980s by my mentor, René Dubos—or a prototype pragmatist, as all climate campaigners like Daniel Sherrell have become.

THINK ABOUT GROWING YOURSELF

I am encouraging training that makes you tough, not just a competitor. To be a "blue-sky optimist" is naïve, if you for-get that walking the frugal line is like dancing on a tightrope above a snake pit. In our approach, you can fall, but you can get up and make the next set of days both frugal and competitive again.

A great change is coming. Powerful social and government movements have taken shape in recent times, calling for a change. This will prove a **golden age in our use of money and rules**, thanks to data analytics and other socially alert management systems on needed **changes in human capital and energy**.

In this book you will learn about corporate examples of climate-oriented projects, as bp goes from a super major oil-and-gas player into an integrated clean energy provider with a host of strategic partners like Microsoft, Cemex, Qantas, and Infosys.

You will also hear of realignment in the consumer-facing firms like Toyota, as well as Unilever, a food and health products firm touching people in more than 188 countries in the world with their Dove Soaps, sustainably packaged foods, and a large train of brands like Ben & Jerry's Ice Cream.

Many remain distracted by the logic of more and miss the creative power in this return to frugality in science, medicine, mining, and technology (even in the children's toys that litter our floors). Those who are leading movements and making change are adept at being frugal. Find here some early voices articulating this golden near-future. In the course of the journey, you will see and understand a better way to use corporate and personal resources.

THE MAGIC OF PRINCIPLES

Organizations run on three basic fuels: **money**, **people**, and **rules**. Spend time learning to respect these realms, not exploit them.

Once you discern the lasting dynamic of these three fateful variables in your life, the history of your life, in a sense, begins.

Consider how the arts I describe and the skills refined in this book make you neither Robin Hood nor an economic fool. Instead, they make you self-actualizing.

Competitive frugality is a fuel in a self-determining world. You cannot control most in your life, but you can shape this realm to your advantage, and the advantage of your friends and family—and, in time, perhaps in your own firm.

These high-octane fuels feed all governments, not-for-profits, and corporations. They form the physical bottom line of our markets, contrary to what your introductory accounting class teaches you. These principles form a triple lens that leads to our near future, much like the ancients' concept of the "third eye" led them spiritually, seeing a set of lasting truths about money, people, and rules.

One principle of this book is that you matter very much in this realignment. You cannot forget people and the rules in the act of making money. As our tutor Ben Franklin states in *The Way to Wealth*, "Do well by doing good." The value of this "alignment" is clear: When you forget people and rules for long, failure is likely. Witness Enron and its many imitators. Witness all the firms that lose their best talents because they do not operate in a socially acceptable way.

The second principle is a fundamental one for the remainder of the first half of this century. **We need to return to a more classic sense of restraint.** Look at our shared needs for clean air, safer oceans, and available lands for food, shelter, and energy. We must learn to be informed, persuaded, and delighted by encountering constraints in this century, just as Franklin was slowly persuaded by the powers in the new world. We live in times of great change.

THE UNIFYING CHALLENGE OF CLIMATE CHANGE

There is one profoundly reinforcing thing about the threats of climate change: many social movements are united under its umbrella of doing more with less.

Climate change asks us to redefine so much: it demands that we think along the lines of this book and realign our sense of money, people, rules, capital, and technological invention. This is because climate change **challenges both the rich and the poor**. The final third of this book explores the plights of children in the vast continents of our earth, as I want you to get outside the box of your own culture and native region, and see that this world needs us to do more with less. This is the crux of the matter on climate change. Pollution correlates to population, rate of consumption, and the grand inefficiency of the petrochemical treadmill from which our original wealth this last century was built.

Another civilizational lesson in the discontent of climate change can be summed up by the paradox of industrial success: **the more you have, the more you are captive to having**. Some in industry now note that the more you have, the more it breaks. This view flies in the face of what our best business schools continue to teach. Our principles test and question the basic assumptions of today's dominant consumer culture.

The last principle, then, is that only *you* can find your competitive advantage for creating wealth. Do not expect your current boss to give it to you, nor your parents, nor grandparents. Do not expect a course on it from formal professional schooling.[2]

Instead, you earn this world view in your daily habits and choices. Our partner in the immersive experiences, CEO Micah Shippee of Ready Learner One, is professionally devoted to helping you certify your worldview in this space.

These principles will help you become adept in the short run and adaptive in the long. A frugal and fair approach to business prepares you for life and family. **It allows you to celebrate society rather than exploit it.** It is in the acceptance of this primal creativity in each of us that one finds true pleasure, true loyalty. **And that is virtually free.** No amount of government regulation or corporate market incentives and rewards will develop those muscles of achieving results in this constrained world. Only you can do that by going back to the classics on social leadership and allowing yourself to enter deep thought.

As We Begin

When you consider the radiance of competitive frugality in your lives, you feel the success inherent in it. You begin to befriend this near future.

Do not think this form of competitiveness is **free from bruising and setbacks.** You will fall, but as you get up with these principles, you will prove more competitive. Like the great game of full-court basketball, the nine chapters represent the ten players in the game, and they all must be in sync

---

2   Business schools are full of cases about teams—and you do need to work with teams. But only you can position yourself and your firm for the more severe future, and acquire the wisdom it takes to succeed. Everything Franklin wrote, with its wit and care, was for you. And you, too, can aspire to that intelligent ideal.

for the game to matter. To celebrate the basketball competitor in each of us, **understand that some players will get hurt**, some **will have only bruised lips**. This is a competition after all, not a great false promise of winning without pain or effort.

This book is about your self-determination in a **world weighted heavily by fate**. The quality of the turbulence you will surf on depends on how habitual you make these principles, and the promise you find in being with your own family, friends, and firms.

When we consider the weight of debt on nations, most politicians only focus on their self-interest and area of control. When we consider how debt takes the radiance out of so many individuals and companies across the globe, we become technical and economical, at best, in our thinking and response.

All experts currently in power must heed the powerful advice given in Franklin's *The Way to Wealth*, or soon be displaced. You'll see his insight goes well beyond "a penny saved is a penny earned," and is worth millions if practiced.

A Way to Sum Up the Overview

In the following chapters we will be exploring the emotional relationships between:

- Self-actualization

- Wealth—both personal and social

- Teamwork

- Innovation and surprise

- The changing needs of peoples in megacities

- The role of capitalism in all this

You will find, by chapter four, examples given from leading companies like Unilever. Here we explore their social genius as a surprising feature on how they compete to do more with less in over 180 countries.

Reading this book is not like going to movies, where you sit to be entertained for two hours, more or less. It will take you a few days in order for it to sink in. It is more demanding than a movie, as the emotions we explore are complex and lifelong.

In addition, unlike a super film, this book is not **complete without your active participation, your reader response**. That is what we call appropriation. I tried to live up to Tom Wolfe's challenge to me by making the book a series of small chapters you could "participate" in. I always believed that participation is what makes the world intelligible.

At times, in the chapters ahead I will insist that something is "stupid." And I will say it is wasteful, and should be ignored. To say "no thanks" to stupidity is another hidden benefit of doing more with less.

Think of the last decades since World War II. We have done so many things wrong in reshaping modern industrial cultures over the last 100 to 150 years that many, many citizens wonder if we can do anything right. If you put trust in the principles we explore in this book, you will make more choices that enjoy results.

You will find a path that fulfills—a path to a new way to wealth.

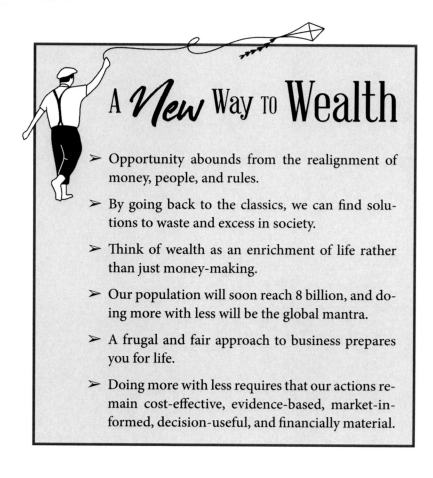

A *New* Way to Wealth

➤ Opportunity abounds from the realignment of money, people, and rules.

➤ By going back to the classics, we can find solutions to waste and excess in society.

➤ Think of wealth as an enrichment of life rather than just money-making.

➤ Our population will soon reach 8 billion, and doing more with less will be the global mantra.

➤ A frugal and fair approach to business prepares you for life.

➤ Doing more with less requires that our actions remain cost-effective, evidence-based, market-informed, decision-useful, and financially material.

Part 1:

COMPETITION THIS
CENTURY

As you read here about knuckleheads, and the freeing attributes in subsequent Part One chapters, coach yourself, and ask how friends can save you at times—from yourself. Find examples of how they helped you save time, money, and waste.

CHAPTER 2

⟨❦⟩

MAKING SENSE OF THE COMPANY OF KNUCKLEHEADS

"But ah! think what you do when you run into debt; you give to another power over your liberty. If you cannot pay on time, you will be ashamed to see your creditor; you will be in fear when you speak to him; you will make poor pitiful sneaking excuses, and by degrees, come to lose your veracity; and sink into base downright lying; for 'The second vice is lying, the first is running in debt,' as Poor Richard says."

—Ben Franklin, *The Way to Wealth*

• •

I came upon an insight about competition by chance. The insight came from watching the smart aggression of hockey. I was drawn into the insight first by watching their fans, both the crazed ones and the informed ones.

My wife and I were enjoying an NCAA final series of college hockey, and we brought our daughter, Colette, then just 12 years of age, to each game.

Colette is now a very hardworking third-year medical student at 25, and married, but I remember that hockey weekend when she was 12 like it was yesterday. In fact, it was a big-time free insight that has lasted and been enriched with retelling.

Normally, the three of us do not enjoy hockey, nor kickboxing, nor boxing together. We tend to admire and participate in gentler team sports, not sports of extreme physical contact like American football or hockey. But a relative gave us special tickets for a playoff series where the quality of the college hockey players was simply exceptional. Rather than awkward aggression, these superb young college players acted like they were born on ice skates. **Their hits into each other were explosively fascinating to us.** And all three of us could see that this took skills of **balance**, **speed**, and **strength** besides simple aggression.

I will never forget the pleasure of watching my daughter get into the sheer speed and talent of the hockey players, so graceful and swift. But our bliss was interrupted by four outrageous knuckleheads.

We had up-front box seats as a gift to the last four games, and these large males were there a couple rows in front of us for all four games. As the best players on the best teams came to action, all four fans became louder and more demanding as the competition intensified—as if their screams and jokes and crudities could summon a fateful result. Soon, in the set of four teams before the final two, these hockey fans were acting insane, banging their heads and hands against the glass whenever opponents skated by, until they were thrown out by well-dressed security guards.

My daughter asked at intermission: "Are they drunk?" I had to say no. She then asked: "Why do they take this so seriously?"

This chapter explores this insightful set of questions from a 12-year-old.[3] Colette was asking the key question: **What is sound competition and what is simply stupid competitive-**

---

3   For it is the sheer opposite of frugality, this knuckleheaded ability to be so wasteful on matters you cannot fully change. Franklin would have encouraged us to explore the limits and boundaries to our competitiveness, as he notes how much we tax ourselves with pride, folly, and idleness. These knuckleheads destroy social value, and litter the way to wealth. They have been so engulfed by excessive competition that they lost their true purpose: to help their team by cheering rather than jeering.

ness? In this book we explore lessons from 20th century social history, lessons about competition and restraint, lessons about avoiding debt yet remaining highly competitive in a daily way. This requires first an **ability to avoid those that will slow you down.** Some call this Stoic restraint, others call it American pragmatism as displayed first by Ben Franklin and then by William James. **I want you to think of it first in terms of the things you learned in the playground of your neighborhood and in sports.**

Photo courtesy of: Getty Images

Before we go much further, I do need to say that I've come to the conclusions and observations in this essay reluctantly, and over a long life. The above glimpse of the knuckleheads may make my point in a visual way, but you really need to think this through more carefully.

Do you really need blue hair to enjoy a game? Or perhaps that tenth beer? Do you really need to be at every game banging your head against the glass?

Our dominant culture, as well as my business and athletic training, taught me to resist this discovery. I was at every game. I did have a host of knucklehead friends, which by chance I learned to avoid before they destroyed themselves. Was this my fate, and how did I sidestep these behaviors for a more productive set of workmanship skills?

From the death of my father when I was three, to the freedoms I enjoyed as a young star athlete, nearly everything I was taught asked me to be self-centered in my competitiveness, to help the world by helping myself first. I think my first half dozen coaches were decent coaches but I watched them behave as wrongheaded coaches at times. I cultivated this more frugal view. They **wanted to win at any costs**, while I had learned from my mother that it was enough to play right, and play strong. I had to learn all this a harder way.

"Social capital"—the networks that involved leaders of cultivated social intelligence like Benjamin Franklin draw on to solve public needs—stands in contrast to self-centeredness.

Many capitalists remain primitive capitalists, people who made wealth with no cultivated sense of giving back. Social capital, instead, involves **shared values.**

Effective leaders cultivate social capital:

1. You see this in those who most often are chosen/elected as the captains of sports teams.

2. Fewer, but some, become CEOs and run highly involved leadership teams of corporations.

3. Others with social value in their actions, in my experience like my friend William Throop, became provosts of universities.

What do these types of noticeable leaders share? **These leaders have the restraint necessary to leverage the social network to the group's advantage.** The second half of this book demonstrates the reasons and appeal of cultural restraint, and explores how it starts with the personal, the subject of the first half of this book. **Without both, you are trying to determine fateful actions with only half a pair of scissors.** You need both to be valued. Once you bring doing more with less into your life, you can leverage that success into your friends, family, and firms. That is the second half of the cut.

What We Forget in Excess

The truth is that we waste most of our youth in excessive competitiveness, spinning our wheels. Like a white-collar criminal, who is always learning to bend the rules, you can get sidetracked in youth by incomplete coaching.

This is not true for all of us.

I had a strong mother who taught me about fair competition. I was lucky in life, being born poor, so I began earning money for my family by age ten, washing whitewalls on cars, cleaning the full cars, and mowing lawns—hundreds of them—by college. When I got to Cornell, I met many people that never worked, and they used higher education as an elite plateau to learn little about work. I come from a different tradition, and have hired folks who find work natural, not something to defer as you exercise the resources of the past.

Pursuing competitive frugality helps you avoid knucklehead behavior, as it sharpens daily habits for team-building and fair competition.

But let's get back to being led astray. I say this now because many business types think they do not need to pay taxes; others think they can bend the rules. Few get away with it for a long time.

Worse, this knucklehead devotion to excess worsens in time—it cements itself to your struggling lungs as you mature into your first to second decade at work—and such wastefulness becomes habitual, like an addiction to cocaine or opioids. This is instead an addiction to idle talk, idle times, and a kind of friendship best left behind. If the self finds its strength through loyalty, lovers, and teammates, then this knucklehead devotion can be forgotten with discipline.

I see this at work in corporate management consulting as well, not just in my early neighborhoods. Some corporate types are 99 percent self, 1 percent social. They will never be embraced through many nations in the nearing future. They may have a short, corrupt run for power, but it is not sustaining. Our century will confirm these principles, as each decade dances into the realm of social response capitalism and competitive frugality.

In the realm of business and sports, some of this self-centeredness needs to be burnt off as we select and settle our identities. But as we age, too often this self-centeredness remains, and we waste effort. We piss away our shared future, acting as active hindrances to the goal.[4]

LESSONS FROM BUILDING A FIRM

I built my management consulting firm by being aggressive in facilitation and by playing hard. Our lawyers and our researchers, our redeployed executives, and our carefully se-

---

4   It is better to be frugal from the start, and hone down our ego. But until recently, I would have never thought that; instead, I was busily cultivating my rather excessive competitive edge. You might have it easier, and may already be sharpening these skills of our near future.

lected staffers followed in a similar competitiveness. We were called fiercely enterprising. The market rewarded us, observing our end product and guessing we had four times our actual shadow of talents.

It is hard to get ahead without competitiveness. But at what cost does it dive into your soul?

But now the confession: I wasted tremendous amounts of time and energy before I learned, in early midlife, how to do the kind of more efficient and more frugal competing advocated in our next four chapters. We now do far more with less: less in terms of wheel-spinning, less in terms of staff, and more in terms of social consequence. And from this, there is abundant recompense with less debt, less risk, and far more reward.

This wastefulness was embedded in the way I was trained to compete. I now see where the crux of true effective leadership resides. **Before it is too late, we must share in the discoveries of a difference between playing hard and playing hurt, between self-aggrandizement and group result.** Creative frugality requires this new understanding of effort. Otherwise, you will keep winning things that do not matter.[5]

In writing my book *Giants of Social Investing*, I was deeply surprised when Jack Robinson noted, "When I put my first million in the bank as a banker, before my mid-40s, I felt hollow." He later got social religion and became a great investor of social good, and what we now call Environmental, Social and Governance (or ESG) investments. But it is interesting that he had to hit that hollowness wall first, being a third-gen-

---

5   Avoid knuckleheads and, instead, find partners who relish one red rose rather than a dozen, who can feel more accomplished in one solid house than by keeping the wheel spinning in pursuit of seven homes. Frugality of effort allows happiness, enables playfulness, and promotes creativity.

eration advantaged person, from his military prep school training through Brown University.

Luckily for Jack and Ben Franklin, they lived long and had a robust second act of great mentoring and giving back. You can learn from this, and do both from the start.

A Gift Available to Youth

Why does it matter how we play, act, and think?

Life, if lived well, can be like a game, but it matters how we abide by the higher facts and rules noted in these forthcoming chapters about scarcity, creativity, and drive.

It matters very much because, in the end, social capital has significantly more value than any measure of financial capital. You can feel reputation and respect far more vividly each hour than the numbers in your foreign accounts. You can avoid tragic falls through succession training and through generosity.

The biographies of those who do more with less—who thrive in the face of limits—are far more compelling to most of us than the lives of billionaires, for example, who inherited their wealth but did nothing memorable with it. Think here about Joan of Arc through the ages, or of Gandhi or Abe Lincoln. **They did so much with so little.** They are frugal, endearing, and enduring social leaders. They stand apart, never allowing the decay of their "social capital."[6]

"Playing hard" is a matter of good old consistent preparation, training, and good sportsmanship. **"Playing hurt" is cheering in the wrong way, like those NCAA knuckleheads.** They threw restraint to the wind, suspending social

---

6   Perhaps it is an excess of professional training; the ease of credit; and the lust for "more" created by advertising that make us forget this gift of youth.

need, casting aside good sportsmanship. Do you see the spectrum of disintegration, or regression into the self, that I am suggesting?

What if we were more frugal from the start? What if we chose, after initial training, to take a job with the new world organizations that value society from the start?

Well, it is often difficult to discern the differences in large organizations, populated as they are by both wonderful, generous leaders and a host of selfish ones. Large organizations like Lehman Brothers and Enron met their ultimate demise from corporate scandal and excess. Later in this book, we will examine superior models of giants like Unilever that, through transformation from their old forms of organization, are making great strides towards socially and environmentally conscious business.

It is harder to discern these "better burning" firms—these stronger momentum players—than, say, watch for scandal: AIG and Tyco are vivid examples of horrible actions. Many can see them as they are burning up.

In contrast, I have come to conclude that corporations that survive over decades have stayed focused on the arts of competitive frugality: they are diplomatic, rather than corrosive. They are supportive of their staff and their partners rather than predatory. You can see this in the second half of the book when we write about Unilever.

And those that benefit from compounded values are social beings, not selfish ones. I have trained myself to look for their values in signing up who to work for, but enough of that. For now, simply look at the good icons, versus the empires of selfish, self-consuming corporations.

Playing hurt is playing wrongheaded. Playing hurt is stupid. Playing hurt ignores the needs of your body and your soul. Too many excessively selfish and competitive people forget these simple reality checks.

Avoid debt, avoid stupidity. Such debt-based stupidity can lead to **your bankruptcy**. I want to pursue a "thankruptcy" for you. What constitutes the absolute worst long-term way to fulfill your firm's destiny is to remain a knucklehead. **Step back from waste, and think.** Ruminate about what works; and now to reflect on what companies serve you, and what companies continue to deceive you and your social needs.

If you allow too many knuckleheads in your firm, in your marketing team, they start lying to close a deal. Look at the damaged icons below: Volkswagen, Exxon, and Shell.

Think about how many thousands of knuckleheads allowed the emissions scandal at Volkswagen. Think about how much wrong was verified by the Dutch court that sued Shell successfully about lying on its carbon emissions. Think through how many thousands at Exxon were doing wrong before a small hedge fund maneuvered this year to have them appoint two climate-literate board members, after years of climate denial and wrong-thinking. If you allow too many unchecked in the stairwell of corporate ascent, then you get the Jeff Skillings of Enron dominating the C-Suite and the Board. In contrast, think through now what you know about these three global ICONS:

Do any of these icons strike you as perfect? It all boils down to questions of degree.

We need improved companies to proceed, but we still need a swift and severe punitive system of laws, rules, and market and capital forces to check the giants of negative social response.

It even gets more vivid. Some firms will go down the S frontier in total defeat.

Witness the bankruptcies of Enron, Adelphi, and select banks in the beginning decades of the 21st century. These are results from when the firms were staffed and led by unruly knuckleheads, such as Jeff Skilling at Enron, a man who made sure the dollar sign reigned high above every one he chose to work with. I remember visiting Enron in Texas during the year before it was "found out" and prosecuted. As you went up to interview "Sir Jeff" in his refined office, you were escorted in an elevator that only reported the news of Enron's stock!

People fill up books with one example of corporate knuckleheads after the other; but to save your mental energy, let me move on.

It is wrongheaded to paint an entire firm evil, or wrong, from bunches of wrongdoing in their divisions. Here is my hunch. The moment people decide to tax social capital, exploit the welfare of their teams, or ignore their fans or their customers, they enter the realm of the knucklehead. When they prolong their demise by playing hurt, there is only loss.

ACHIEVING RESULTS

So how can we achieve results in a changing world?

In order to achieve a satisfying solution to our desire to compete, in an overpopulated world, we each need to reach for frugality.

You need to realign money, people and rules, accordingly. That is the first step past the knuckleheads, I believe.

Money, People, and Rules

Those are the magic variables that prove fateful for non-profits, charities, and especially for mid-sized to large corporations, the kinds that I've always consulted for.

I call these the three "fateful" variables: money, people, and rules. You need to develop triple competencies to thrive in competitive frugality. You do not need a graduate degree in Finance to develop the core basics of financial literacy, such as the avoidance of debt and the wisdom of compounding money in the bank. The next chart demonstrates why this urgency for re-balancing is a physical result of population density.

World Population (in Billions): 1950–2050

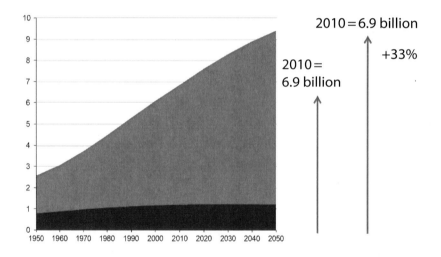

In my prior books, *World Inc* (2007) and *The Surprising Solution* (2010), I explore in detail how corporate behavior is changing in a world filled with almost 8 billion people.

But, in retrospect, I did not pause long enough to explain in those earlier books what truly distorts and disrupts real competition in firms. You can see this disruption occurring now as many global majors announce their pledge to meet net zero carbon emissions by 2040 or 2050. It is far too easy to change the public relations and the lobbying tactics than to change your staff and the machines of production.

Two things have changed since those books on globalization and social needs, and these two torrents of change are what inspired this new investigation.

First, several of my clients asked my firm, from 2010 to 2021, to start benchmarking how companies as great as Toyota and bp got it wrong regarding their social risks. (bp experienced a $26 billion loss in value from its Gulf Spill, while Toyota had a massive vehicle recall over a leaky fuel tank mishap.)[7] Even well-run giant firms misstep—that is the point. But the larger point is society notices, and slams them in time.

You cannot get away with too much knucklehead behavior if you are going to serve your stockholders, and answer the scrutiny of your key stakeholders and employees.

Second, I began to answer the requests by giving my clients Jim Collins' recent book, *How the Mighty Fall*. This served as a great holiday gift to key clients as my firm approached its 30th anniversary in 2011. It has become more valuable as a gift book each successive year. In this short, significant book, Collins notes how hubris, arrogance, and a blind faith in endless resource spending often put major success stories into bankruptcy. After robust success, soon they wanted more. Why?

---

7   This "ask" for more on Enterprise Risk came from client firms as big as the CEO and CFO of Warren Buffett's Shaw Industries, key leaders at Hess, the new Chairman at FMC, and a key engineering SVP at ConAgra. We also heard it rumbling among our ongoing 40+ Corporate Affiliates. This caused some pause (and some pain) in our staff and our Senior Associates, as well. We realized something in struggling with these questions about anticipating enterprise-wide risks: as a firm, we were hitting all the pistons when it came to the major market-shaping shifts we had become known for. But when it came to ranch-betting actions, we were only beginning to understand what good governance required.

Well, again, the answer was serious shifts in history, and the expectations of citizens. Since Jim Collins wrote his "enterprise-wide" work on *How the Mighty Fall*, we have experienced several global financial meltdowns. The person on the street now knows how excessive debt and poor governance explode. My clients felt that they needed to get to what was the very rotten core of this problem. Calling it the celebration of greed was too simple. They needed a framework, based on a humanistic insight, that exposed many, not just elites. And I tended to agree with them.

Enterprise risk is best governed and managed not from the top down. It is not really a technical engineering protocol, nor is it a formal governance challenge, as still suggested by *Directors and Boards* magazine or the *Harvard Business Review*. Those high-seat views miss the real causes of the scandals.

In more technical books, like *Wealth and the Commonwealth*, that will follow this current volume, I will explain more on how to govern and manage enterprise risk, which enables an important step forward in corporate behavior. I call it social response capitalism. The current reader is given the logic on personal and lived experience terms; but keep in mind that enterprise risk is on a global corporate scale similar to the competitive frugality you need in running your own life.

The more I began thinking about this, the more I realized knuckleheads had become elemental in business, almost universal in the spectrum of industrial activity after World War II. We had evolved a set of rules that allowed them to walk halls without transparency, without accountability. What was ailing advanced capitalism was its senility: It forgot the ever-vital link between competitiveness and frugality.

IN THE COMPANY OF KNUCKLEHEADS

To put this boldly, we have far too many knuckleheads in business and in sports today. They waste our social frugality, and much social value. Some have the calm and confidence of well-paid fools. Many are loud and many wrong. None are easily corrected or easily realigned to task.[8]

For some reason, it is easier to spot knuckleheads among sports fans than in business. But after 40 years as a management consultant, I can assure you they thrive in modern businesses as well.[9]

We unravel this phenomenon slowly. It has crept up into our midst, into our headquarters and regional offices so quietly and so cleverly over time. It needs to be cut out methodically—like the stinging layers in a most ripe onion.

A NEW WORLD

Today, in the new generation of specialized organizational communications personified by Dr. Micah Shippee in his firm and in his introduction to this book, there are better ways to hire talented staff and train their social intelligence on the job. This is what firms like bp and Unilever do well. I will explain that more fully in subsequent chapters. For now, know there are different animals in the zoo of the global mar-

---

8   A reason my profession of management consulting will never die, and does quite well in stressed times in all economies, is that we are taught by experience how to catch and throw the spears that eliminate knuckleheads for management. The leaders know there is a flood in the basement, but they use us to weed out and mature up those that are keepers.

9   Who are these knuckleheads? They are the guys and girls who stage highly visible raids during well-attended corporate meetings in support of some highly inconsequential item. They are the opponents of the frugality of effort. They fight for a fleeting kind of attention at headquarters, to serve small ends. They simply cannot enjoy a game of serious strategy from afar; after a certain point, they must thrust themselves into a smaller kind of game.

ket, and some will thrive while others will lose based on the principles I am outlining in this book. There will be a vast middle landscape as well.

When looking for a visualization of what competitive frugality looks like, think about Michael Jordan. His competitiveness was visible, shark-like in its efficiencies and team play. I've written a book on this, *Doing More With Teams: The New Way of Winning*. For now, I could not have done that without first embracing the principle that doing more with less is success. Jordan won seven championships by noting this fundamental necessity in basketball: the lasting competitors learn to do more with less.

For me, the key theme here is that many of these corporate and sports knuckleheads are playing hurt.

They deserve your help as a teammate or captain. They are crying in a sense for it. Their behavior is based on their underestimation of the value of social capital to their lives. They have lost social perspective. They take risks that hurt themselves and the society itself. In this profound way, the game of life replicates the games of our competitive youth.

FROM GOOD TO GREAT TO EXTREME

What does this tell us about competition today? Our culture continues to allow these people to rise in fame and stature by an excess of competitiveness. That is what I mean by "playing hurt." There is a profound difference between playing to win, within the rules of the game, and playing hurt, or cheating.

Knucklehead thinking is neither good nor great.

It is about the excessively competitive self. They no longer question themselves and ask: "Am I interfering with my neighbor's pleasure in the game?"

Or: "Is it possible that my actions will be perceived by my family and friends as questionable?"

Instead, some pee in the gas tanks of their opponents' parked cars. When asked why, they report, with a deadpan kind of humor, "Because they have the opposing team's insignia on their back bumper."[10]

But here is the bad news. The vast majority of those populating the firms of today are not addressed by Collins' analysis in his three great books.[11]

I cannot report, yet, on the rate of knucklehead thinking in the modern corporate mansion. But I have seen boards

---

10 In sum, this is a bigger, deeper corporate and social problem than those addressed by Jim Collins in *How the Mighty Fall*. For it involves the common man and woman, not just the greats. Jim, the expert observer whose Good to Great remains at the top of the Christmas tree of all business books year after year, outlines in his most recent book the five stages of decline. This sounds about right to me, in my experience—but these five stages of decline only matter for no more than the five percent of our corporate people, the ones making the key decisions. Jim is exactly insightful for CEOs, CFOs, COOs, the profit and loss leaders of the business units, and sometimes he is keenly insightful on the aerodynamic drag found in technical executives and general council staff.

11 When a firm is beginning to descend, well, that's when leaders need to forestall further error and get everyone back into work. Jim now talks of success as luck, because so many of his early cases have been dated fast. He seldom descends from his data-rich celebration of competitiveness to ask about knuckleheads in the firm. Peter Senge and the legend Peter Drucker are different in their worldview than the competitive Jim Collins. Drucker was far more like Franklin, witty and aware of human stupidity, and was quite keen on the stupidity of excessive competitiveness. Senge is hypersensitive to these issues, to the point of being ineffective in groups. The answer is somewhere between these great minds, back in basic ways of reward and guidance to our staff. Drucker and Senge, and many others, have pursued the difficult thought paths of unlocking the real sources of waste in a firm. Jim focuses at the competitive top, which does not represent more than 3 to 7 percent of most modern firms in my experience. And when you get to non-profits, the problems are far worse.

swayed by similar behavior of chairmen, except that their knuckleheads did not involve any body parts.[12]

Whether man or woman, whether primitive or advanced, how the mighty fall, in my books, involves a switch in one's head that allows an escalated sense of self-worth in determining the outcome of a game you really do not control. It is as simple as that.

OUR PRIME EXAMPLE

Rather than paying the price of knuckleheadedness, you can stand on the shoulders of giants like Gandhi, Franklin, and Lincoln, and better your lives almost for free. This takes the formula above: you need to blend analysis, or a situational awareness of the game, with sensible reliable action. The result will be compounded value both in your pocketbook and in society. You can travel widely through relatively inexpensive books, as Lincoln did to move from the hinterlands to the White House. You can choose winners by being more selective, rather than building an immense staff.[13]

Frugality and restraint are the name of the game in constrained formats. Think here of Japan, and Germany, and the

---

12 When I say body parts, by the way, I am writing about a paradox in modern life that includes both sexes, in my experience. I know woman that have tattooed the name of their firm and the name of their team inches above their breasts, one above each breast! I work out with women, each day, that say life for the firm is more valuable than life in society these days. You may know many men who have sacrificed commonsense and restraint to tip their hats at an Enron-like excess. Perhaps I am being a bit sportive here, or excessive in my rhetoric, but I do not believe I am stretching too far. Woman and men have fallen prey to knuckleheadedness since World War II.

13 You can earn your way to second base by steady practice, not by running bare-assed like Mr. Coakley, or by hiding the numbers like so many of the corporate leaders now in jail. Eventually, it will feel good when you round third, fully dressed, and walk your way home with result and social value in hand.

way Brazil and China must become in short order. There is simply not enough time and resources left.

Walking Home

The art of competitive frugality is what sets you free. But if you forget to be mindful of this, it is so easy to fall further and further from home. I am not reciting the medieval virtues of prudence here, or age-old lessons from religious texts. Instead, I am writing a song of commonsense.[14]

In sum, we are all in the company of knuckleheads. They are abundant in modern society. They often descend into the delusional. We must reform their ways. In times of wrong, you cannot find a solution by only looking at the top of organizations for all the answers. The answers reside in your choices regarding money, rewards, and rules at every level of your organization.

The answer resides in correcting excess.[15]

---

14 After three books, the clinical psychologist James M. Glass summed up his experiences with psychosis in a telling paragraph. I offer this densely written excerpt to reassert the central kernel of this essay, namely—we know when someone has wronged society, but it often takes plenty of labels and words to find out exactly what is wrong with them: "It is my belief that participatory power cannot be maintained without constant struggle against the tendency to fall back toward delusional or psychotic states in the self, particularly delusional time.... This effect of the self to maintain a psychologically secure reciprocity and mutuality indicates a set of psycho-developmental transitioning from narcissism and omnipotence to consensual reality, or the world of society, law, and historical conceptions of time."

15 That train of self-aggrandizement moves incredibly fast. But what is really unstoppable is frugality. It wins out on most trips. Frugality is unstoppable because it becomes more relevant in time. Whatever happened to this grand old Earth can be remade anew only through frugality.

Knuckleheads, now in retrospect, appear to me delusional. It is just that I tolerated them more. I now see this in the four men at the NCAA hockey game; in John Rigas of Adelphia; Jeffrey Skillings of Enron; and Bernie Madoff of the investment community.

Whether you are a principal in a rural high school, a person developing a new firm on micro-finance in Africa or Latin states, or a modern relocated corporate middleman in New Jersey, you have a job before you—so cut the knuckleheads before they cut you.

This takes more than you think.

A *New* Way to Wealth

➤ We must burn our self-centeredness, and stop wasting time, energy, and resources.

➤ True leaders understand the difference between playing hurt and playing hard. They gain more value in social capital than any amount of financial capital.

➤ We need to find our competitive advantage through a more frugal path.

➤ Knuckleheads disregard the value of a social network. Leaders gain more value in social capital than financial capital.

➤ Truly impactful people like Franklin, Gandhi, and Lincoln were frugal with time, resources, and friends, which made their ascents possible.

➤ What are the habits of success? Knowing you need to align money, people, and rules in your teams, you then need to place clear objectives of fair competition before each, and then trim the performance. This is quick, reliable on-boarding in today's swift world.

Prepare to think about what loyalty is in your life, what provides satisfaction. Then use this chapter to tie them both to your sense of hard work— hard, industrious, socially valuable work. This forms your first team, along with your family.

CHAPTER 3

THE NATURE OF WORK:
LOYALTY AND SATISFACTION

"Sloth makes all things difficult, but industry easy; and he that rises late, must trot all day, and shall scarce overtake his business at night; while laziness travels so slowly, that poverty soon overtakes him. Drive thy business, let not that drive thee."

—Ben Franklin, *The Way to Wealth*

. . . .

We only have a finite number of acts to realign our money, people, and rules. Life might seem long, but Time is short, and each day valuable. Youth and early maturity give you trial fields to compete in; before you are in bigger leagues. If we fail to respond to developing the muscles of fair competition, you can enter an entire stadium of stupidity. Keep hydrated and aware of how big the stadiums of life can become. Come prepared, my friends. You can win far more than you lose. You can secure a winning position within the clearing given to you by time.

Photo courtesy of: VitalikRadko | Depositphotos.com

In this next essay, we remind ourselves of the inventiveness beneath scarcity, its lifelong logic and impact, and ask: What are the finest examples and principles of competitive frugality? Why might it prove our best means of survival and success?

Photo courtesy of: Peter Feghali | ExploreCams.com

Often our sense of a buffer in our life is delusional. Yet in fact there is a small empty space of grace around you that manifests your chances. But it is not forgiving, nor is it immense. You might do best to practice hard before you perform. We think we have many friends in the stands with us when, in fact, our friends themselves have the space to compete before them. We think we can hide behind a Stanford degree, a high-tech market, a bubble of real estate deals, but we cannot hide any longer in waste.

A Case in Point

There is a man I served, Pat Mahoney, who gave me a great clearing to succeed for him. Pat Mahoney had graduated a generation before from the engineering firm I taught at for a decade—Rensselaer Polytechnic Institute (RPI)—America's first engineering school.

Pat watched quietly, as I spent three years developing a Master's of Science degree program there based on the dual competencies of science and engineering, with the leavening of management savvy. You can think of it as a 45-credit Master's graduate program that is more rapid and more applied than the generalist MBA programs. Once I finished the degree, Pat called me up and said: "You'd better be good at this. I want to hire your best students." He was one of the CEOs that hired my best students from the program. He was a keen competitor who became a friend and a generous supplier of income to my firm across decades.

I served Pat early in my career until late in his. The former CEO and founder of Energy Answers International, he was a frugal client. I had served him and his global energy development company for more than 18 years before I learned, in an interview for this book, that he was a devotee of Ben Franklin, and that "doing more with less" was the enabling mantra of his life. I say all this to you now in full honor of his remarkable life, as he passed away in the middle of the second decade of this 21st century, after we did a number of astonishing gigs together.

When we talked at my office, Pat spoke about "discovering" Franklin's autobiography when he was a young engineer in school. He described turning the pages with a "strange awareness" of "what Franklin was going to say next about savings, about frugality. I knew then what I wanted to do with my work after school at RPI," Pat said that day. Pat remains the only CEO of impact that took the time to visit me in my own offices. He was that way!

Since reading Franklin's autobiography, Mahoney has built a number of enterprises, including an engineering firm (Smith and Mahoney), and Energy Answers International. I have had the pleasure of visiting him in his founding office across decades. Like a fine wine, the room is the same, the leader is always alert and clever, and the process of learning how he thinks and works gets enriched with time.

Pat Mahoney

Mahoney made the pilgrimage to Franklin's birth home in Massachusetts at mid-life, and has made many visits to

Franklin's digs in Philadelphia and to the Franklin Institute, a museum devoted to science education. Obviously, this CEO is as much about a frugal worldview as building large and effective machines, and it has served him well.

Below I chose to display the range of his accomplishments by a single billion-dollar project: his sale of Energy Answers' SEMASS project to American Ref-Fuels.

SEMASS (Southeastern Massachusetts Resource Recovery Facility) was Pat's baby, a waste-to-energy and recycling facility located in Rochester, Massachusetts. He designed it, matured the hundreds of staff members, earned the licenses to operate it. My role was to help Pat lead the team, as he grew it from 2,000 tons a day to 3,000 tons. At that point, he used me to build a bridge to the buyer, where he sold it at a rich profit, sharing with me abundantly.

By burning processed waste at the right temperature, residence time, and turbulence, the SEMASS plant sold for decades reduced-price electrical power to the Cape Cod area and the local electric utility. In time, as part of his dream of a renaissance in the harbor area, Pat managed to sell excess steam to a maker of fibers and then the U.S. treasury.

Another project—not completed due to his untimely death in his seventies—was an astonishing "eco-industrial park." He had designed one for Puerto Rico, and another for Baltimore Harbor. But again, the weight of time left these undeveloped. But my point is clear: start early in your pursuit of frugality and invention, as even a great life is short.

Some reporters called any of Pat's plants the product of a win–win–win approach. Some felt him "dangerous." I call it a master plan based on insights into frugality and social capital. Mahoney is competitive in a smaller world. Before his death, he sold his concepts to Island economies like those in Japan.

As we shift your focus on thinking about Pat Mahoney as not only my friend but as a CEO who brought me and his firm great wealth, let's begin to think about Nature and *Natura* of our species in an ecosystem.

Well Beyond the Mean

What Mahoney did forty years ago with Energy Answers in Albany, New York, and then again in SEMASS, is appropriate for all megacities. This case points to the lasting differences between playing hard and playing hurt.

If you are hurt, you expend more effort, and you play inefficiently. But if you play hard and creatively, it is frugal. It is today's equivalent to how Franklin conceived the first public library. You need to balance the efficiencies in self-interest with the long-term social needs. That is Mahoney's exemplar genius.

Mahoney feels Franklin taught him how best to involve many different kinds of people, and obey many rules, on his way to substantial money. "I find you can do more by saying less [being concise] most of the time. It is profoundly important to be underestimated in all negotiations," Mahoney noted, defining yet another feature of competitive frugality.[16]

---

16 I came to the same conclusion as Pat Mahoney about disclosure, but after many sad and excessive failures. In some ways my stoic silence now is based on a midlife crisis, of sorts, where I had an insight into the nature of competition in smaller, more severe settings.

Now that we have 6.8 billion people on earth—all competing for food and energy, and forced to choose between the needs of industrial transportation and the net decline in arable land per citizen, I find that the insights articulated here have helped me develop my personal and corporate strategy in the world I described in my last two books. We need, in a smaller world, to operate well beyond the mean. Achieving trust today requires a demonstrated care for the near future.

Fast Back, Before We Fast Forward

What do we mean, exactly, by "social capital," and why does it matter?

Voltaire, French writer and 18th century philosopher, aptly noted, "The art of medicine consists of amusing the patient while nature cures the disease." This is far more frugal than the modern approach, where excessive insurance allows undue risks, and excessive interventions prevail. No set of surgeons can successfully cut away the habits which manifest obesity and hypertension through expensive surgical techniques. It requires a more frugal behavioral set of changes to repair the patient.

My school of management consulting is based on a stiff and stern parallel to Voltaire: "The art of good corporate governance consists of healing people and their spend of money and rules in a corporate mansion. In these acts you find a frugality that cures any disease in business." You call this simple. I find it effective.

Many are beginning to note: What ails the modern corporation is its robust ability to do too much.

The successful corporation learns to do more with less, which is the stronger, lasting foundation of success. Nowadays, I find it more profitable to say "No!" ten times to each "Let's see."

Here is the ugly part. With machines the size of towns, and consumers anxious to buy, a large percent of the modern corporation's mansion is built by people separated from the real choices that matter. They are doing a lot that doesn't really matter to the core positioning of the firm. And, worse, in their silos they are quite isolated from the market shifts and value shifts in society. As we move to a smaller world, it is important to keep all this waste and disconnection in mind before you start the cure.[17]

A DECLARATION OF INTERDEPENDENCE

If our system remains swift and severe, as I predict it will until at least 2050, we will become even more interdependent with each month. This makes me think back to other turbulent days. Early in the drafting of the *Declaration of Independence*, Thomas Jefferson wrote of letting "facts be submitted to a candid world." Jefferson spoke of pledging "our Lives, our Fortunes and our sacred Honor" to a greater cause, and he revealed why we must not spend our energy on wasteful anger and bickering but instead invest in the future.

I reread federalists like Jefferson and Franklin whenever I tire of the day's Washington, D.C., bickering on TV—all that mindless wheel-spinning.

---

17 Some economists and politicians think that a discovery of this degree of waste in the modern corporation will pop our economy like a dried balloon. These are the folks that say "more lean" is too mean. They argue we need a company's excess, that we need excessive supply-side economics in order to grow. I know them to be wrong. The best jobs are in doing less, and from firms that subsequently survive over decades.

Jefferson knew that there were clear enemies of the old before his brethren. He was bold, and wanted us to remain bold, remain self-sufficient. What that means for competitors today can be seen through the lens of the Babylonian Talmud's commentary on the classic Psalm 128: "Who is rich? Those who are happy with their portion."[18]

Rock-solid Examples

It is easier to see the exceptional in art than in an industrial plant like Mahoney's. Let's examine the phrase "well beyond the mean." By that I mean anything that is visibly exceptional. Here we refer to the things that society comes to favor over time.[19]

Frugality exists every day in how an exceptional leader spends their time, how they allow or disallow the wastes of knuckleheads. It is evident in products that survive the tests of time. The things I really treasure I've had for at least three decades, some four. These products stand against planned industrial obsolescence.

Some call this exceptional success "creativity": the ability to do something beautiful and valuable with less effort than your competitors.

You can find rock-solid examples of frugality near you every day. My wife would rather have one red rose on a special day than a dozen. Each year she buys a smaller Christmas

---

18 See https://reformjudaism.org/learning/sacred-texts/learn-about-middot/contentment-ones-lot-middah-samayach-bchelko

19 The phrase might describe an exceptional investor or an exceptional stakeholder in the environmental community. It could refer to a capitalist with a reputation for innovation, like Steve Jobs or Pat Mahoney. Or it could characterize high achievements in a specific field, from industrial chemistry to carpet manufacture. I found observations and principles "representative" of frugal leadership skills.

tree, so we can note excessive gifts. She helps us to lavish gifts more on others in need.

If you compete properly—and if you are generous in sharing your gifts with friends, staffers, and even competing firms—you amass a great deal of social capital in a short lifetime. Thus, "well beyond the mean" also implies the ability to create a buffer of sanity—a "social cloud"—around your firm and yourself in this rather turbulent and vicious world.

To help you visualize this link between exceptional behaviors and social capital, we start with an ancient idea—stone carving. You do not have much time to waste in stone carving; and your fingers get fatigued when you waste the gestures.

Photo courtesy of: Techninjas | Zuni-fetish.com

Think now of a stone fetish carved by an expert Zuni craftsman. It is exceptional. These southwestern stone fetishes you can see and feel in airports: they are rock hard. They withstand the wear and tear of being displayed, handled, and packed in a suitcase for the trip home. They are beautiful, and they are dangerous.[20]

Once you visit the dusty origins of these products in the Zuni lands in New Mexico, you realize that the terrain has been profoundly misnamed: This is actually *old* New Mexico. Some say the Zuni have been carving these stones for 5,000 years.[21]

The ancient families still in touch with the traditions, such as the Teddy Weahkee family and the Theodore Kucate family, have brought their art into modern global life. Their works have made it to Calgary, Paris, and Istanbul, and I believe I once spotted a Zuni family icon in Kyoto.

My point is simple: whatever the native American artist is capturing in a piece of stone—whether a game animal, a domesticated animal, or a corn maiden—there is something simple, magical, and compelling about these fetishes. Think, then, of the idea of making better products, or a better firm, by using less stone, as frugality.

This helps me see what is so special and exceptional about Pat Mahoney's industrial ecology approach. He is using less of his resources to make power and value for others. And imagine, if you will, how urgent and necessary this combination of

---

20 While I can see why some want to spend $20,000 on a lovely necklace for a wife or lover, I have never spent more than $300 on a stone fetish, a rate of pay per hour of our Senior Associates since a decade ago. That is the limit I find pleasant for a non-essential. Of course, you need to find your own balance here, or those credit agencies will know you too well.

21 On a personal note, I love the badgers, wolves, eagles, moles, coyotes, bobcats, snakes, and owls. Lately, I have been seeking out the frogs and turtles. As the real frogs of this world seem to be disappearing more rapidly in our severe circumstances, I wonder whether, a thousand years from now, these fetishes will be our descendants' understanding of a frog.

social capital and frugality is today, as we pile mountains of waste around the ordinary. The 21st century requires that these imperatives be accomplished at once. We have real options.

FINDING LOYALTY, THE MOST SOLID STONE
IN ANY FIRM AND FAMILY AND FRIEND SET

There is an antithetical relationship between mean staff selection—what some call "state-of-the-art competitive hiring"—and commonsense loyalty. Loyalty turns out more profitable and more sustaining associates. My most loyal colleagues are exceptional. The Yale attorney Ken Strassner has been loyal and productive for over 18 years. In today's turbulent world, that is exceptional. Can you see why I failed in my selection of some veterans from JPMorgan, or when some of my best-trained folks left for Goldman Sachs? Loyalty is as precious as a Zuni stone, and arguably even more rare as a trait.

Photo courtesy of: Texas Children in Nature Network

At this point in life, I see the loyalty in my staffers. They conserve by taking public transportation instead of the limo or the hundred-dollar taxi. They carry out important results one quiet day after the other, efficiently moving forward, achieving social results. Achieving results through loyalty is the flip side of avoiding knuckleheads. You become a magnet for efficient performers. I hope you find this importance sense of loyalty; it does not cost much. Loyalty is another benefit of doing more with less: when your staff sees the owner is frugal, and not wasteful or showy, it is easier for them to think of saving the next dime.

LOSING GROUND

I would be lying to you if I said there was this richness of loyalty from the start. There were years of waste, years of stabbing competitiveness. And yes, years of wrong hires.

But what I have found is really quite possible for you now. You stop losing ground when you stop spending energy on wasteful gestures, arguments, competitive fights over price. You need, instead, to master your craft like a Zuni stone worker. That is to outsmart the higher facts of scarcity.

This is not the same as the traditional recommendation to "work hard." **Working smart is about not working against yourself, or your loyal colleagues. It is about doing more with less.** In contrast, too often, in modern capitalist settings, we mistakenly believe we need to be mean and fierce to get there.

You know the gruffness I refer to here: from the plane to the train, from the banks to the law offices, we see the damage inflicted by those who lack civility. This hardness lurks in the shadows of most negotiations and is why Harvard Business School Press has an entire bestselling series on how to deal with difficult people. Avoid all that.

Most firms that succeed want to attract a frugal set of leaders, a small band of teammates. True enough. And I add to this that in the end we need to withstand the test of time, like a Zuni fetish. Do not lose ground in hate, greed or regret. Greed is the most infectious vice. Regret is a form of advanced self-pity. Play a more frugal game next season. Avoid the wheel-spinning, avoid the knuckleheads in your firms, and find a group full of creativity and loyalty. This gets us much closer to the purposes of money. It opens doors to creativity and satisfaction, when engaged frugally.[22]

The Purpose of Money

Money is not only about money, or the making of more money. Money is about respect, reputation, and revenue. So where did we go wrong? Where did all the knuckleheads come from?

Today, if we asked the best-trained MBAs from INSEAD in Paris or from Wharton, Thunderbird, or Harvard, "What do we mean by 'money,' 'commerce,' and 'company'?" they'd say, "I have no clue. Give me the money." Why have we gone senile as capitalists?

We must combat this cultural senility by realigning the roles of money, people, and rules for our new century.

---

22 My friend, Bill Shireman, the founder of The Future 500 leadership network, ends each email with this quote: "The moment one definitely commits oneself, then providence moves too. All sorts of things occur to help one that would not otherwise have occurred. A whole stream of events issues from the decision, raising in one's favor all manner of unforeseen incidents and meetings and material assistance which no man would have dreamed would come his way." Bill and I have learned, through experience at many firms, a deep respect for a couplet often attributed to Goethe:

"Whatever you can do, or dream you can do, begin it.
Boldness has genius, power, and magic in it. Begin it now."

WELL PLAYED, BEN FRANKLIN

Ben Franklin left $2,000 to Boston and Philadelphia to help young people in those cities. But he stipulated in his will that the cities could not draw the balance for 200 years. By 1990 (the bicentennial of Franklin's passing), the bequest was worth $6.5 million. The money has been used to fund scholarships, women's health, and financial assistance for firefighters and disabled children.

Be like big Ben and think about compounding value in the future, now. In the last chapters, we will describe the urgency for this realignment.

Historical accounts show us the real roots of business and money. In ancient Greece and Rome, for example, money came from "the goddess of relationships"; in Latin, "company" meant those with whom bread is broken.

Before the advent of oil and the abstract instruments behind derivatives and high finance, most cultures defined "companies" with a sense of this human and biological scale. Business, in this way, proved as basic as breath.

In this context, a company is conceived as a social response to opportunity in a context of real scarcity. You succeed because you are doing something better, with less waste, than your competition. There is a social satisfaction in knowing this is the essence of a good business: it resides here, in a set of rock-solid principles. We end Part 1 with a hint: Once you understand your role in addressing the tangle of social needs, you have many options before you, and another way to wealth.[23]

23 For more, please visit my page on *Medium*, where I write about the accomplishments on social change found in the great films by Spike Lee (https://brucepiasecki.medium.com).

    As you relax and watch any film of substance and drama, think about the nature of work they will teach you about this chapter.

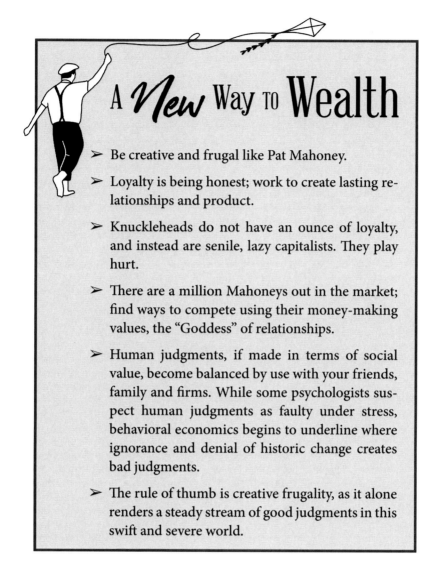

A *New* Way to Wealth

➤ Be creative and frugal like Pat Mahoney.

➤ Loyalty is being honest; work to create lasting re-lationships and product.

➤ Knuckleheads do not have an ounce of loyalty, and instead are senile, lazy capitalists. They play hurt.

➤ There are a million Mahoneys out in the market; find ways to compete using their money-making values, the "Goddess" of relationships.

➤ Human judgments, if made in terms of social value, become balanced by use with your friends, family and firms. While some psychologists sus-pect human judgments as faulty under stress, behavioral economics begins to underline where ignorance and denial of historic change creates bad judgments.

➤ The rule of thumb is creative frugality, as it alone renders a steady stream of good judgments in this swift and severe world.

This next chapter examines healthier forms of competition. Consider the bleakness of not responding to the carbon and capital constraints we share in our combined near future. Avoidance of this climate and capital challenge is not sensible. Denial is proving no longer tolerable. You need to be more artful, more competitive, more frugal on these central issues of our century.

CHAPTER 4

c%⌒

THE ART OF COMPETITIVE FRUGALITY: THIS CENTURY'S WEDDING OF SCARCITY AND CREATIVITY

"Lost time is never found again; and what we call time enough always proves little enough: let us then up and be doing, and doing to the purpose."

—Ben Franklin, *The Way to Wealth*

Time is always short; and of this Earth the "Anguish—absolute—And many hurt," to quote Emily Dickenson. This social awareness of the *natura* of life actually constitutes the opposite of stupidity. To acknowledge, with alertness, the anguish of the world, and how many people are hurt, is the birth of social awareness.

When we contemplate the power of responding to scarcity with creativity, we begin to refine the coordinated muscles of competitive frugality, this new yet ancient metric of personal and corporate success. Stupidity, or the refusal to see that the world seeks frugal social responses, is a new form of historic denial. I've come to think of a competitor's stupid shots, or mean traits, or self-destructive behaviors as signs of an auto-immune deficiency in their brain. They are thinking they have an endless life to waste. Wrong, most every day. Like a 48-minute basketball game, life is measured and short. Take frugal shots, share the ball, be a team player.

Stupidity is the art of denying reality. (Garret Keizer notes it is "The Third Force" in his opening essay in the September 2021 issue of *Harper's Magazine*.) Stupid, Garret notes, "doesn't mean unintelligent or even uninformed."

Keizer goes on to argue it means a losing your grip on historic actualities and social change, where a stupid person blinds themselves into a false certainty.

The Nazis could only prevail for as long as they did because of all the stupid "compliant" people that followed their hate. It is healthier to recognize these people of harm and hurt as "stupid," as wasteful of the richness in the shortness in life, When I experienced first-hand Donald Trump and his people—like Steven Miller (the architect of his anti-immigrant white supremacy)—I found them to be fundamentally stupid people. I believe history will confirm my instincts. The things Donald Trump said throughout life about whites and "them," the things he said about hoping the Russians had Hilary Clinton's emails, were simply stupid.

What is worst is the massive waste he created in the prejudice and anti-immigration patterns of his followers, who had to take deliberate steps to deny reality. We are a nation of immigrants. The world stage is full of devastation. You cannot wall off a nation.

They wasted so much time building a wall, so much good will hating. Their time in power was short lived, like the Nazi regime, yet sufficient to cause real damage. Sure, those four Trump years proved horrible for many; yet enough reacted by mobilizing to defeat his massive war chest of hate and isolation.

Yes, it was bleak. I thought often of how Trump's policies would impact my foster brother Edwin Torres and my Asian-American sister Susie. You can see why millions of good people came out to defeat this monster. Those that denied historic reality, for the short-lived advantages of racial prejudice and perhaps some miserly tax advantages, were defeated in the popular vote. I use this example not for political reasons, but to talk vividly about what I mean in this book about the tone and the voice of social change.

I speak this strongly about Trump without being overly political. I vote Republican and I vote Democrat, depending on the good values of the candidate. But again, this chapter is about social trends and social history, not my preferences.

In a future chapter, you will see how the global brand-based company Unilever responds to the social change agenda with great profit and good, while others become isolated in hate, bias, and wrong-doing, like a petty elected official.

But in the end, my argument is more than personal: there is a wedding of good will to be had when we confront the scarcity of life. When we are open to the diversity and social needs in life, life itself affirms creativity. This is why I am naming this part of the book **"Fate Respects Frugality."**

All great literature dances from this awareness of our mortality. And what is the source of social responsibility? It comes from transacting more with less in the context of hurt and anguish. You can take this as a marriage of historic trends, and a marriage of necessity to facts before us.

The classics often remind us to do more with less. When we recognize the shortness of life, the emphasis is always on the smart doing, and the saving of time and effort, without becoming machine-like. Stupidity can prevail for a time, but not for long.

Franklin sees a brilliant string of pearls connecting diligence with the elimination of distraction, waste, and self-harm. I have argued the same, yet added some modern context based on first-hand experiences in executive coaching and management advisories. If only our great competitors of tomorrow can keep Franklin in their cubicles, we'll have better products and a better world in this time of competing for sustainability.

All this takes a marriage of good and evil traits, a balancing of the worst in competitive natures with the best. I find the first route that trained me, and my best hires, in this area involves repeated assignments that marry scarcity with creativity. I argue in the chapter coming up that Unilever is a remarkably frugal firm, people-affirmative, and competitive. Unilever is provided as an example of a firm that understands cognitive sciences; they market products that have become accepted as eponymous.

But I am not claiming this as the only way to success: via massive global institutions. You can get there on your own in a small firm or family business.

In other words, if you deliberately excel with a self-limited budget, and can explain to your superiors how you got your result by saving them money, you win. The art of competitive frugality involves the musicality of this balance in the score. It is not only about direct points, but all the things the basketball player embodies—as a minute-by-second transactional player—besides scoring, like handling the ball, the exact pass, the best defense. Capitalism is foolish when it only looks at the scores, rather than what I call "the momentum fundamentals" described, rather casually, in the tales and details told in the coming pages. I find that world soccer dramatizes the same principles in Latin and European audiences as what I am now noting about well-played basketball games. Like the market, these games reward and respect team play, team coherence, the sharing of shoulder strength over knuckleheads.

THE HEALTH OF PEOPLE

The magnificently complex health care legislation of the world is not my expertise. Although I've advised the top 30 executives at Merck (from the big pharma side) and Walgreens Alliance Boots (from the pharmacy distribution side) for the four years around Covid-19 and its challenges, I still feel this realm a complex one. I say this to suggest perhaps your career can be centered on bringing the tools of doing more with less into this incredibly inflationary realm of the global market, from UK's system to the States, and those I've experienced, by chance, in my travels.

Health care embodies the compromised but effective ways in which complex balances between the price of drugs, the accessibility of care to the elderly and the poor, and the need for constant innovation in a world of mutating viral threats must be achieved, monthly, if not annually. Think again about the complexities embodied in that balance.

Today's smaller world requires practicality, such real politics in both business and society—greater frugality in governments, corporations, privately held firms, and in the management of your own nest egg. For only frugality guarantees what Einstein has been attributed to have called the greatest human invention: compounded interest.

Through an intense full-court press, our world leaders need to work the media, capitols, opponents, and the industry coalitions to get what the majority of people, not just the rich, need in affordable health care—from Africa to the States. The net effect: more citizens will need to have access to health coverage. But all of us will have to see key privileges and significant extras cut from our benefits, like the sizzling fat from our morning's bacon.

I say this as well from the advantage of being on a Board of Directors at the Medical Consortium on Public Health and Climate Change. Here we hear the concerns, and the practical decision points, of all the major medical societies in the country, and in some cases, through benchmarking, in the world. I leave these Board meetings, held by WebEx every six weeks, with the uniform underlying feeling that the entire medical system must learn how to do more with less.

RELATE MEDICAL CARE TO CLIMATE CHANGE

Look at the facts of climate change. Elements of shared risk, like hazardous waste, toxics in ground water or now greenhouse magnifiers in our atmosphere require comprehensive multi-national "showed" responses. Health care reforms follow this pattern too. I sum up our shared grievances here. In the bullets prepared by our key Senior Associate and **Yale attorney Ken Strassner**, you see the parallel between health care and climate change:

1. One degree Celsius of warming has already occurred in our shared atmosphere due to the petrochemical

treadmill of the last one hundred years. These are verified man-made inputs versus pre-industrial levels.

2. Business-as-usual implies further increases from 2.5 degrees Celsius to as much as 4.0 degrees of warming by 2100, the natural length of my daughter's life!

3. Significant social impacts have already been baked into our industrial responses and government policies, such as responses to droughts, fires, stronger storms, and cargo lost.

4. The critical response time to "build back better" with less is now to 2030. Thus, the timing of this reminder book.

5. If warming can be limited to 1.5 to 2.0 degrees by 2050, major new additional severities can be largely avoided by society. This is why firms like bp and Unilever are so aggressively transforming.

6. The best routes to eliminating further emissions are the lessening of the use of fossil fuels like oil in transportation. Other large routes of productive reform are being secured in the electrification of buildings in megacities throughout the world. There is room for additional efficiencies through the use of smart data by firms like Flex, Siemens, and other business-to-business giants in automating and electrifying farming and industrial processes.

7. *A New Way to Wealth* can help corporations in their climate expertise to see the bigger picture, and to calculate their form of social response capitalism. Corporations can also advance society through their adaptation and resilience plans, readying for the fires and floods expected in select regions.

8. Board members, CEOs, and CFOs need to understand these issues and closely supervise corporate performance to win these areas covered in this book, and many others.

The time that board members have to read these materials on public health and climate change is increasing. It is the new bottom line. These shared grievances underline the need for globalizing the principles in *A New Way to Wealth*.

The surprising social and industrial lesson from this change: most of us learned how to spend less on health care. If you eat right, exercise, and avoid a set of severe proven vices, you can extend your life and thus productivity—the morale and motivation behind doing more with less. Of course, we are aware—as caring professionals—that all cannot follow that self-determining path. The invalid, those that suffer and survive strokes, the aged—we need our complex system to support many. In fact, I think the Covid-19 pandemic helped many realize how generally supportive of society the health care system can be, even as it underlined the vast sections of society underserved in terms of access to health care.

Where can we find the answers to the third medical industrial revolution now required? If you read the medical histories, as I've begun to scan after joining this Medical Consortium Board, you are humbled by the complexity of the system.

This does not take more money to resolve, but more discipline. To date, if we track each White House public briefing by the Centers for Disease Control and Dr. Fauci's explanations to the press, and correlate them to parallel policies in Israel, Sweden, and Mexico, we learn a lesson in which political compromise, complex deal-making, and awareness of capital constraints brought all of us into a more frugal way of dealing with our shared future. In the end, Public Health solutions are solutions in society asserting how to do more with less.

It is important to explicitly note that in this climate of political division, frugality is not tied to a particular party and its beliefs. In our nation's largest challenge this century, the Covid-19 pandemic is our case-in-point on how we become creative in response to scarcity and severity. Although not a perfect set of outcomes, our public health world experts and decision-makers debated on Covid and its variants for the two years I've been working on this manuscript. Each month we learned, collectively, how much relief was needed and possible, and what was excessive. As I prepare this book for publication, we still need much work on the pandemic in Africa, Asia, and the developing states of the world, including the failed ones.

Fast Forward for a Moment

By now you can begin to comprehend the complex set of emotions called forth by what I have named "the art of competitive frugality." In the last chapters, I will begin to tie these observations, both personal and professional, to the new discoveries about hope and the human brain. The fields of big data and cognitive sciences, after 300 years, now underline much of what Ben Franklin preached in his aphorisms that have lasted the test of time!

But what exactly do I mean by this alluring term, "The Art of Competitive Frugality"?

You can view the definition of this art in practice by going to www.AllAfrica.com, where you'll find thousands of artful cases of women and men putting frustration behind them and discovering you can deliver milk without the spillage of sachets.

AllAfrica reports: "The outcome of watching so much spilt milk is an injection-molded 'Clip-It' sachet jug. This is designed to hold a liter sachet of milk securely and at the exact angle need for mess-free pouring from the source." Thousands of gallons of milk are now not wasted via every use in Africa that is alert to this new frugal device. E.F. Schumacher called these frugal ideas "technologies with a human face." Those with the eye for frugality know that their value is greater than the milk saved.

Another area of the world to explore: greater Asia. You can get the definition of the art of competitive frugality in practice by going to www.NYTimes.com and putting the word "frugality" in the search box. From India to Indonesia, from Malaysia to the immense continent of Australia, you'll find examples of productive thrift. While this chapter has focused on American health care, in particular, the principles are global and universal to other areas of management and your self-actualization.

THE RULES OF THE NEAR FUTURE

Now let's return from our fast forward to the issue at hand: how best to preserve our vital resources for the future. I first wrote about resource wars in my 1990 book, *In Search of Environmental Excellence*, with the California journalist Peter Asmus. I mention this because the reviews of the book, after it won the Nature Society book of the year in England, came out in "moral platforms" like the *Christian Science Monitor*, although the book's reach was into more secular categories. This I found odd. Is it only those of "moral" aptitude that worry about scarcity, resource rules, and the finite nature of critical minerals, I asked at the time, rather naïvely? Now more than 33 years after that book, I can ask, "Who should *not* care about limiting their consumption of resources in this time of climate change?" Yet the question of rate of consumption is always still a "repressed" matter in many technical and financial circles.

We are on a treadmill in a sense. Yet there are a number of new world rules pushing the capitalist and the consumer off this treadmill.

Decision-makers—from CEOs to the leaders of nations—are finding new ways to do more with less. They are cherishing their seed-corn, not spilling it. In a real, pragmatic, day-to-day sense, frugal decisions each day add up to your successful quarter or year, not the year itself. View your staff like the man holding vital grains; be warm to them, not exploitative, like a Trump.

Of course, harsh behavior and retaliatory, predatory behaviors allow you what in basketball games we called some "earned elbow room." But in the end they do not win games. The game of life requires diplomacy, loyalty, and the sharing of team wealth.

You cannot proceed in its denial in your life. And these are the rules of competitive frugality that are shaping more and more lives in the near future.

History gave us early exemplars. They are animating the essence of Abraham Lincoln's letter, detailed further in *Lincoln on Leadership* by Donald Phillips, in which Lincoln writes, "My policy is to have no policy. I shall not surrender this game leaving any available card un-played. **I shall do *less* when I believe what I am doing hurts the cause, and I shall do *more* when I believe doing more will help the cause.**"

Lincoln allowed himself to be persuaded upon being better informed, much as today's decision-makers must do with their alignment of money, people, and rules.

If you think about seed-corn, and how keeping it primary and replenished—as seen in the gesture described a few paragraphs below—you realize this has become a daily prayer in a sense. We must all think about a near future collectively.

The reason is simple: There are many more of us—7.8 billion at least—in this smaller world, where we must share our health care, our milk, and our products. And since we all consume more than our grandparents, often by a factor of 20, there is an urgency, even a new nobility, to this search, one that isn't exclusive to CEOs and leaders of nations.

In this smaller, 21st-century world, we must all become like Ben Franklin all over again. Blending frugality and industriousness is more primal than technology for technology's sake, or more science "because it can be done." We must face these higher facts of scarcity and creativity in a frontal way this century: the age of consumerism is giving way to a more creative age of conscious restraint.

THE PATH FORWARD IS TOGETHER

The former provost William Throop centered his college on educating to this end. He noted that as we encounter limits, and successfully outmaneuver them, "the world becomes more intelligible...we feel accomplished and satisfied because to participate in a larger social journey, with a set of smart competitors, makes us grow."

"Humans are hard-wired for this kind of competition," Throop—a calm, meditative leader—continued; "and I've come to believe that the logic of frugality is our path forward together. Over time, over the next two decades, frugality is the central rallying call that will bring forward both leaders and new potential in the new generation of designers, thinkers, and doers." The brilliance of our species is in our hard-wiring for competition; and testing limits, we can push the effects of our collective restraint and frugality to the max.

Throop defines the rich domain of this next chapter with his latest book, *Expressive Rightness and the Fidelity of Proper Thinking*. While we start the inquiry on health care in an over-populated world, we are extending the example to be more encompassing of competitive frugality in general.

ARE THESE NEW RULES HIGHER FACTS?

We have suggested that the common universal appeal of being a knucklehead no longer works. It is idle, destructive play. We have also suggested that there is a series of things out there for your frugal use—like expressive rightness and the fidelity of proper thinking. You may be asking at this point: Does this set of artful skills constitute a way of the world that replies to something in society—like an image of fate—that is larger than mere markets and money-making?

We'd best think this through now before we address the more complex issues of personal signature, brand, and innovation.

For years experts measured how the world was muddling toward frugality in terms of gross domestic products, the health of economies, and through our rate of consumption. These studies are usually empirical and trend-based. But we want to focus on a set of higher facts that define the world we now live in—whether rich or poor, whether industrialized or aspiring to be industrialized.

These are the higher rules that enable a fully formed leader to be creative in new constrained situations and down-turns, and that allow new-century beginners to take leaps forward when they rethink their future. These are the rules about frugality and competitiveness that define our new world of scarcity, where water and land and food and energy are more precious than ever. Let's view this as a positive social result of the last 40 Earth Days.

In the two exhibits that follow—one that displays how stakeholders like investors and rule-makers have redesigned the modern corporation to be osmotic—you can see into the corporate mansion and ask it the kinds of questions you ask yourself and your friends. In the first image we display this new swift world as the S Frontier.

Here in a nutshell is why I think it pays to consider the rules of frugality as a set of higher facts. The world has become swift and severe, that is for sure. Most of my clients understand that at midnight, at midday, or at 6:00 A.M., when they start in the megacities of this world. This swift and severe world forms a new S Frontier, where most are driven down the S into pressured lives.

But some that are frugal, creative, and clever—what we used to call street smart—start to rise on the S Frontier. I have seen that again and again in leadership circles.

For those firms that are rising on the up end of the 'S,' we call them momentum stocks. That is, they have some technical, terrain, or human talent sets of advantages that allow ascent rather than mere descent or steadiness. A game is not a steady-state thing; it is fast, ever-changing in score and momentum, and that is what it takes in today's world. See the way this exhibit from my book *World Inc* relates the everyday dynamics of the swiftness of information and the severity of market conditions into a new form of social response capitalism.

You may now begin to contemplate how the arts of competitive frugality allow you to enter into the stairwell of a corporate mansion. Each firm in this world is in the market, in the middle of the S Frontier, and each firm is full of a mansion of talents and people.

Yet for years I did not pause long enough to contemplate the full meaning that the power of the power social change had on the value for a firm. There are winners and losers in this globalized capitalist world. The social safety net is less derived from governments than in the past. It is more the result of global firms like Unilever, bp, Google, Amazon, and Apple. You need to be a weaver of that net for yourself, your career, and your family before it begins fraying in your life. The best way to do this is to do more with less—that is, to save a certain percentage of your earnings from the start to compound value and safety moving forward.

Yet here is a higher fact: We live in an age of "social response capitalism," a world where we compete on price, quality, *and* social needs. That is where the successful reside. If you accept this as higher fact, you begin to ascend into the new century.

For now, let's simply keep the basics in mind as we relate most of this book to personal self-actualization, not organizational strategy.

WHO RUNS THE WORLD, IF NOT NATION STATES?

What have I learned from watching President Obama, President Trump, and now President Biden—as well as the other elected leaders I see, from Turkey to the Latin states, properly reported on the BBC world news?

Not as much as I learned from watching the great corporations over the past ten years, as they responded to the needs of today. If you look at poverty, disease, and the strains on water, land, and forests, you will see that governments and nonprofits frame the questions that corporations rise to answer. It would be naïve for me to claim all corporations provide answers to our mounting social needs. And it would be wrongheaded to appear as a corporate apologist here.

I am a corporate change agent. The record on Wikipedia in my name, and in the books, illustrates the difference. I am pleased how the public world of Wikipedia is judging me, but the new generation and the press are those that need timely new answers to an endless stream of new conflicts and new issues. This is how the world turns. My point is that we need an entirely new generation of writers to cover how business and society co-evolve, and how one force challenges and benefits the other. The answer requires those two halves of the same pair of scissors.

The last 20 or more years require us to learn the classic art of frugality all over again—and apply it aggressively in industrial cultures. This demand for civil coherence and competitive frugality has reshaped politics, corporate life, and your nest egg in the blink of a few years. There are many who have lost their shirts and pants in ignoring these historic shifts by keeping the declining assets of politics or corruption in focus.

I see this ESG investment trend as the great differentiator in corporate and political life. Those that acknowledge scarcity and social needs begin to prosper as the selfish are perceived as no longer momentum bets by investors. Now, this higher fact did not come from national leaders. It is a newly extraordinary feature of modern advanced industrialism and our global equity market. While the evening news entertains us with talking heads of little long-term consequence, the quiet insistent call of frugality rises in its cadences. Corporations fail, and governmental administrations (think Trump here) are voted out, when they are not accountable to social solutions.

Why does this matter?

Well, if we fail to adjust to this higher imperative for competing on frugality, we will feel the severity of limits squeeze even stronger. If we do not make the necessary shifts in attitude and values, the fabulous complexities of money will continue to baffle and hurt.

Many Americans mistakenly believe that when it comes to complex issues—from fossil fuels to immigration to health care—we can bring about the necessary changes through regulation alone. But regulation is not enough in this carbon- and capital-constrained world. The corporations get this—at least the best ones do. Rules are part of the grand mix that allows the flow of money and the rise or fall of people.

We must go lean as we go green. We must go global, as this inter-connected world is far swifter than our best thoughts. It will punish the wasteful, and waste the wrong-headed knuckleheads over time.

Witness the seat belt, witness the rules on eliminating wasteful light bulbs, and witness the way CO_2 is being regulated by the EPA in the U.S. in the absence of Congressional alignment. Early adopters shape possible and needed change; and then, rapidly, money follows the opportunity in the new, more demanding rules. That is the way of this world.

This is why we need to become Ben Franklin all over again. (Forgive me, but some things are worth repeating.) In the coming decades, we must become incredibly inventive in developing new forms of energy, and incredibly frugal in our investments.

To achieve peace, prosperity, and health, we must develop and disseminate the art of frugality. The well-dressed ambassadors of frugality must offer this logic as the long sword of our politics. This is the hymn of our work days and our nights.

IF THOUGHT RAN THIS ZOO

With the foamy tempest of this new century still roiling its salt and spray before us, you need to look ahead with the resolve of a lone fisherman in a storm. The best in us will bring forth this artful frugality. Punch right now the word "frugality" into Google, but make it regional. Put in "frugality/India." "Frugality/Indonesia." "Frugality/Asia." "Frugality/Africa." You will be surprised by the wealth of example you'll see in action. What I write about is common sense, but it is the kind of common sense we do not see until we ask these questions about fair competition and social need.

Before my death, we will see rapid and contentious legislative changes on big issues like carbon taxes, renewable energy portfolio requirements, and tax requirements for excessive luxury purchases—what the Romans of yore called *Sumptuariae Leges*, or sumptuary laws, designed to prevent inordinate and ostentatious expenses in food consumption and dress. Today most states and provinces in the world are reducing the barriers to cleaner energy efforts, from battery infrastructure to renewable fields. They tax waste.

If thoughtfulness ran this zoo, we'd have all that we need now—from Turkey to Texas—but tomorrow will tell more. There is a "last-party" mentality in some powerful, resistant forces of society, yet I see them losing their grip each week.

Already, I can foresee by 2030 large urban towers, sky-scrapers of food production, to outsmart our imbalances on food for more people. To visualize how much room we have to grow, consider this image of food production in our future:

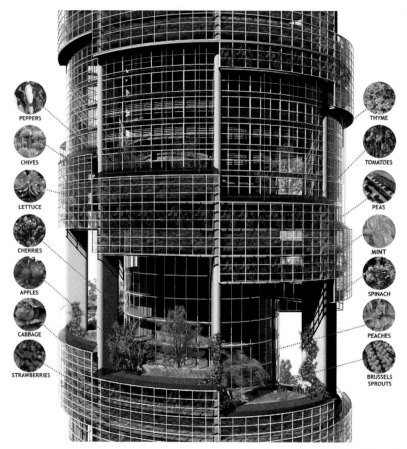

Photo courtesy of: Blake Hurasek

And then look at the recent *Fit for 55* climate package[24] agreements in Europe. Here, 27 nations have articulated a patch to reduce in nine years their greenhouse gas emissions by 55 percent to 1990 standards. When I first wrote about a prudent policy for climate change mitigation in my 1990 book with Peter Asmus, I never imagined that all of Europe would agree to set 1990 as the reduction standard. This takes a doing-more-with-less mentality.

While there is still much to be done, already I see rapid progress in renewable energy (back in 1990, renewables were exotic, meant only for tree-huggers and extremists; now they are the basic essentials at most utilities of consequence), as the net production of conventional oil continues to decline annually. Already I see smarter products like electric cars, less toxic metals in computers, and more efficient homes. This is only a start. **What matters now is you.** You can sense the larger wave mounting, if you adjust your thinking.

This type of change of giants will soon cascade on down to all Profit-and-Loss leaders, and this will green the most reluctant CFOs and COOs. That means all corporate leaders who get the need for sustainability now will rise as the others fall. **This is a swift and severe new truth.** Markets will reward those that come first to the idea that there is less arable land per person to achieve sufficient food and energy supplies. It will involve rapid, important shifts to alternative fuels.

In short, I predict that a single theme will dominate our next decade in business and society: We will need to do more with less.

---

24 See https://www.consilium.europa.eu/en/policies/green-deal/eu-plan-for-a-green-transition/

Further Reading on These Predictions

For other examples of frugality in action, visit these online sources:

1. https://AllAfrica.com/

2. https://MoneyShow.com/Investing/

3. https://www.TheAsiaNews.net/

4. https://www.TheReporterEthiopia.com/
   (select English as the preferred language)

5. https://JakartaGlobe.id/Opinion/

6. http://www.BusinessAndEconomy.org/

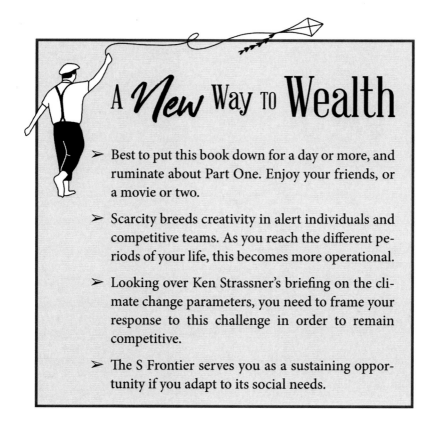

A *New* Way to Wealth

➢ Best to put this book down for a day or more, and ruminate about Part One. Enjoy your friends, or a movie or two.

➢ Scarcity breeds creativity in alert individuals and competitive teams. As you reach the different periods of your life, this becomes more operational.

➢ Looking over Ken Strassner's briefing on the climate change parameters, you need to frame your response to this challenge in order to remain competitive.

➢ The S Frontier serves you as a sustaining opportunity if you adapt to its social needs.

Part 2:

FATE RESPECTS FRUGALITY

In Part Two chapters you will see how a company can integrate social trends and social history to run with frugality and social expectations in mind. You will see how your company can help in the process of greening other firms while helping the youth of today and future generations to focus on a better planet, marked by less inequality and a better standard of living.

Wislawa Szymborska is a globally recognized poet of our day. I use the following poem of hers to suggest that fate respects frugality.

TWISTS OF FATE

A Poem by Wislawa Szymborska

It may have happened.
It had to happen.
It happened before. After. Nearby. Far away.
It happened—just not to you.

You lived through it because you were in front.
You lived through it because you were in back.
Because you were alone. Or with others. On the left. On the right.
Because it was raining. Because it was darkling.
Because the weather was sunny.

Fortunately there was a forest in the way.
Fortunately there wasn't a tree in sight.
Fortunately the glass, the hook, the beam, the brake,
    the doorjamb, the bend, the millimeter, the second.
Fortunately you spied a blade in the water.

Consequently, because, and yet, despite,
    what if a hand, a leg,
    a step, a hair's breadth
    from coincidence.

So are you here now? Or still stuck in that happenstance?
The net had one opening, and that's how you got through?
I can't shake myself from it, nor shut up about it.
Listen,
    how fast your heart beats in me.

(Translation by Frank Weaver)

CHAPTER 5

∽⦾∽

INNOVATION AND THE
ELEMENTS OF SURPRISE

"We are taxed twice as much by our idleness, three times as much by our pride, and four times as much by our folly."

—Ben Franklin, *The Way to Wealth*

. . . .

The folly of seeking more science, more medicines, and more purely technical fixes is that you never get there. You never realize you've been lucky until you know how to declare, "Enough!" Or, "No thanks." Or simply, "Let's proceed, I have work to complete." The mantra of "More is more" is a damaging path of excess. It consumes the lives lamented when William Wordsworth wrote, "Getting and spending, we lay waste our powers."

This is basic physics (and basic economics), which we sometimes forget. Our approach offers a set of actions and principles that become more important in contexts of increasing scarcity, with *A New Way to Wealth* based on surprising frugality as a path of compounding innovation. In this chapter we disclose parts to the puzzle of the mammoth global firm Unilever to illustrate some key elements of surprising solutions before us.

As the world's population grows from 7 to 9 to 10 billion people this century, intelligent tradeoffs on food and energy will become second nature. Franklin wants you to leave the market of old industrial ideas seeking more and more, and return, when appropriate, to the wisdom of doing more with less.

In rethinking these classics with me, I hope by now you feel like you are sitting near a friend. This offers you the creative license to reignite your prior self and help it rejoin this new world.

How I Got Lucky

I have been lucky in life. Having been born poor, in a house where my grandmother coped without medicines through advanced age, I learned early the skills of doing more with less.

These early experiences sat on my head in a classic fashion, bringing wings to my early experiments, as they were all based on competing with less from high school to college to my first jobs. I began work at ten years old on my birthday, and I still enjoy daily work at sixty-six. I have always found joy in earning and loyalty in sharing.

Even when earning less than $10,000 per year as a landscaper in high school, I saved 20 percent of that annual income "in case." Sure, my mother was dirt-poor after the death of my father, and I decided pebbles were worth keeping "in case" I would never get anything bigger. During my ten years at Cornell University, I spent much less than my scholarships, buying used books and used clothes. Sometimes mocked by my peers, this unusual behavior still left my mind enriched with quality movies and plays and good friends. That is when I started saving in a grander fashion through TIAA-CREF. Soon enough, in a matter of 2.4 decades, the compounded value of our holdings set my family financially free. If I had lived higher on the hog, this would not have happened so early in life.

LEAVING UNIVERSITY LIFE
TO BECOME A CHANGE AGENT

In my first two professorships, tenure came fast but my reluctance to feel secure led me to maximum tax-deferred annuities (what a wonderful device!).

By the time I was in my mid-forties, I could do the math of financial independence, and celebrated silently the power of compounded interest and tax deferral. I was an early investor in a tax deferred annuity at the Teachers Retirement Fund (TIAA-CREF). In fact, my selection of "social choice" funds paid off substantially.

The trend continues as my firm now earns millions most years, globally, from sources as diverse as Merck, Walgreens

Boots Alliance, Shaw Industries, and the host of 32 other companies listed as Corporate Affiliates at www.ahcgroup.com. I say this with a sense of loyalty and humility each week, since we tell our clients to fire us without notice if we fail to serve them. We have no debt and thus no interest payments—and I say this with a sense of gratitude and humility; since we could not have done it without the principles first instilled in our actions by the writings of Ben Franklin, Marcus Aurelius, and the other compelling authors noted in our Appendix.

What stayed constant in all this was my love of people, my respect for frugality and freedom, and my sense of how rules can be reshaped into creativity in times of stress and scarcity. I wrote this book lens reflection so you can rejoin that world if you wish. It really doesn't cost that much.

A TRIBUTE TO THOSE THAT SHAPED ME

For those who want more of this personal side to the argument, please consider getting ahold of my memoir, *Missing Persons*. I do not want to say more than it was through friends, family, and my firm that it all came together, like concentric circles in the same pond.

And for those who want this principle applied to some of the world's largest and most successful firms, I've applied our book lens and themes to a publicly known global firm, Unilever, the food/beverage/brand global giant. I have to do this as part of a public puzzle, as I never worked for Unilever. In them I see confirmation of what I anticipated in prior books and prior management consulting assignments—but even larger!

For the founding Lever brothers were known to be frugal, competitive, diplomatic, and Franklin-like, which is a talent selection process of renown at this successful company. Just as Dizzy Gillespie knew how to choose the best balance in his band, Unilever puts together astonishing teams, and then trains them to address social needs.

I have lost two young, talented staff members to Unilever, as they pay well, and are actively mentoring. I will refer my briefing soon to William Novelli, noted by CEO Shippee in his introduction. Novelli became the master of social marketing; and he got his feet wet first at Unilever. In thinking about this living legend, Novelli, you can see why work on social action pays.

THE ELEMENT OF SURPRISE

A personal strategy of acquiring a reliable brand, like a big Ben Franklin, is not very much unlike company brands. Fierce focus on consistency is an element; yet so is surprise. A surprising personality like a Lincoln, an Aurelius, or a Franklin is also in some sense first a consistent branded one. I will go to jazz legend Dizzy Gillespie to demonstrate this point, at first counterintuitive but wound tight into to lives of those who compete in a frugal, reputation-based way.

One AHC Group experience that sticks in my mind—because it exemplified a wonderful use of the element of surprise—was by none other than the renowned jazz trumpeter Dizzy Gillespie. Dizzy surprised myself and other business owners and attendees in the Washington Park area by agreeing to play there for the community *for free*. Dizzy did more than just entertain the community, but spiritually joined it, by using the element of surprise.

As someone who donated monies for this free concert to the Albany League of Arts, I was a sponsor among dozens at this event, in the company of nearly countless music lovers.

Dizzy invited me backstage with a purpose. He wanted me to stand with my basketball shoulders and a few other donors as "false bodyguards" around him.

He had some members of his entourage drive very slowly a mysterious white Cadillac with tinted windows around toward the back of the park by the stage, which was visible to the crowd. I was stationed stage-side as a bodyguard for this entrance, but I could see the Cadillac crawling up the side of the crowd of thousands.

The crowd's fixation on the car, and the anticipation of him emerging from it, meant few realized that Dizzy himself was making his way to the stage opposite from the car, wading through the crowd from the back.

He jumped up on the stage and said: "Dizzy is my name and jazz is my game." Now that is a man who knows how to play by the score, and still delight and surprise. I want to leave this short chapter reminding each of you to keep an element of surprise in your day-to-day.

Now to leap forward: What is the closest global firm that embodies this jazzy sense of social and productive surprise? I would vote for Unilever, the maker of over 300 world-adopted brands like Dove Soap and Ben & Jerry's Ice Cream.

THE SOCIAL GENIUS OF UNILEVER

In this chapter we will argue that Unilever's sense of social purpose is broader and much deeper than the buzzwords flitting around "Corporate Purpose" and "CSR." All corporations have the purpose of making money; but those that integrate social trends and social history can expand their margins. This is the compounding effect of Social Response Capitalism, and the engine pulling Unilever's 300+ brands. In fact, visualize

Unilever as a large Japanese bullet train, with social response the fuel, and each cargo car and its internal compartments run with frugality and social expectations in mind.

Before we get into how Unilever utilizes a completely frugal and cognitive science view in their product adoption, let me sum up why I believe they are a social response capitalist firm:

1. **Social Response Capitalism remains a vital part of the present, and future, of corporations.** Social Response Capitalism provides firms the license to operate in many corners of society—from food security to personal hygiene and health products—ensuring that they maintain that ability to grow through frugality into the future. This explains why Unilever has products sold in over 182 countries in the world; and is ranked as the number one employer of choice in each region of the world. Unilever is a firm that competes as a social response bullet train, responding to changes in social expectations regarding sustainability, climate change, and social inclusion and cohesion on a dime.

2. **Social Response firms do not fall prey to deceptive and vague notions of "corporate responsibility."** Instead, they set their social aims, profitability, and talent pools around social trends more lasting than market trends like carbon and reduction. As women are being empowered, they empower women. As climate change is becoming first and central, they got to over 38 percent renewable across the world before I began writing this book three years back. Any non-business social historian can clearly see that; but only a few firms, like Unilever, Iberdrola, Trane, bp, and Merck

see the fuller impact and opportunities of Social Response Capitalism.

3. **"Sustainability" is not the only social issue at hand for Unilever. They have aggressive renewable energy achievements and climate-reduction goals.** That is why their surprise is to remain frugal about finance, innovation, and competitive advantage. In my client work, I sum up these findings in the six elements of corporate transformation. This forms a solid, impressive response to carbon and capital constraints.

Corporate Strategy, in this new world of big data social expectations, takes responses to *panic* with *resolve*, the two forward-looking features of the human psyche. These forward-looking features help Unilever pick talent, winning partners, and allies.

This is a new world where Business-to-Business alliances prove mission-critical to success; and Unilever is a vivid example of this.

SELECTION OF UNILEVER BRANDS

Here is the fun part. It pays to study Unilever's brands. In most cases, people do not know the holding company Unilever, but 95 to 98 percent of most European, American, and Canadian households are familiar with at least several of the Unilever brands that follow. My household is fond of Vaseline, Q-Tips, Dove soaps, and about a dozen others shown on the next page.

Look in your kitchen and bathroom cabinets and discover the social genius of Unilever.

ON
ANY GIVEN DAY
2 BILLION People
in 190 Countries
Use Unilever
products

OTHER
GLOBAL UNILEVER
BRANDS INCLUDE:
VIM, SUN, VIA, BOVRIL,
BECEL, CORNETTO,
IMPERIAL, JUST FOR
ME!, POT NOODLE

SOME OF THE FUNDAMENTALS

Unilever is the second-largest advertiser in the world after Coca-Cola. But they do it more effectively based on social data and social trends, not hard-armed spending. Nuanced ads in different regions of the world work for them, in the same way Ben Franklin changed his persona in France from that of Philadelphia. This is not lying; this is doing more with less.

When they put Sustainability at the heart of their operations, it grew their business, as they were fueled by competitive frugality in each region of the world. What follows demonstrates their ability to hew to the principle of Chapters One to Three in an integrated fashion, repeatedly.

They took clear actions on Covid well before national polices, caring for their immense staff, providing tests, time off to get vaccinated, and team alignment sessions. This embodies social response capitalism.

You can see their aim, like that of a Ben Franklin, is to inspire other companies. They know that social expectations are larger even than they are! There is a kind of capitalist humility, a Franklin-esque diplomacy, in keeping that humility operational at Unilever.

THE REACH OF UNILEVER

The following list, on its face, doesn't seem to indicate doing more with less; it portrays, in fact, a very large company. But you do not get this large through waste nor with knuckleheads.

- **2.5 billion** people use Unilever products each day

- **400+** Unilever brands are used by consumers worldwide. In our analysis, about 80 of them are primary in results and revenue, but they are always experimenting.

- **190** countries in which Unilever brands are sold include most of the world; and their penetration into the wellness market matters to many of their buying public.

- **155,000** Unilever people deliver this global reach efficiently. They are far bigger than most firms in employment status before governments and regions.

- **€52 billion** in turnover in 2019, when we shared their data with our Corporate Affiliates in a series of intimate benchmarks.

I cannot overemphasize the importance of frugality in running over 300 brands in the firm, for each product is treated as a separate profit-and-loss entity. Think of each brand as a business unto itself, sharing the insights of the entire giant on social change and a social need.

This is their popular mantra, repeated: "Our brands give us a **unique opportunity to create positive change**, to grow our business, and to achieve our purpose of making sustainable living commonplace." Unilever relentlessly repeats its core messages in at least 120 countries. They know enough about the landscape to not advertise relentlessly in some of their countries, unlike the more wasteful Coke, which spends bundles everywhere.

THE PUBLIC HEALTH BEHAVIORAL ELEMENTS OF THEIR GENIUS

Unilever's grand global reach provides them with a huge responsibility *and* a huge opportunity. In learning the power of doing more with less, this kind of social responsibility is felt daily.

Unilever brands focus on helping consumers improve behavior and develop good habits, e.g., regular hand-washing, reducing dietary sugar, etc.

Unilever identified five metrics necessary for these behavior changes to take root:

Understandable	Easy	Desirable
Rewarding	Habit-forming	

These relate to social behavior, not just consumer purchasing patterns; they *are* the social contract.

There are seven kinds of brand science in practice, according to our AHC Group internal tracking systems, and Unilever synthesizes them all.

Furthermore, Unilever supersedes these with a neuroscience synthesis of "concept" and "social" brands.

THE UNILEVER SUSTAINABLE LIVING PLAN MADE SIMPLE

The Unilever Sustainable Living Plan centers itself on a **profound social paradox**: "Doing More with Less."

"The Unilever Sustainable Living Plan sets out to decouple our growth from our environmental footprint, while increasing our positive social impact." I will not spend much time explaining their piece of the puzzle, as many others have done this part of the Unilever story. Go see the publication *2020 GlobeScan SustainAbility Leaders Survey and Report,*[25] for instance.

Instead we focus on elements of surprise:

- Their commitments span critical social needs and environmental and economic performance indicators across the value chain.

---

25 https://globescan.com/2020/08/12/2020-sustainability-leaders-report/

- Their genius involves many others. They focus on partners and areas that drive the biggest change and support the UN Sustainable Development Goals (SDGs).

- Unilever measures include percentage of renewable
energy used; mobility and food programs for need; and
aiding social stability measure.

- They have a transactional code of behavior for each region of the world. This means that they measure the
social value of their products before and during their
transfer from manufacturing to delivery. They refrig-
erate in a social sense their product brands.

THE TRICK IS IN THE PARADOX: "DOING MORE WITH LESS" IS THE KEY TO SUSTAINED COMPOUNDING VALUE

Listen to how they plan to make sustainable living more
commonplace over the rest of this century. You can pull swiz-
zle straws—competitive frugality—to see each piece of the
fabric below. I share key points from thousands of discussed
pages:

1. Their sole business focus on **long-term growth** provides benefits to Unilever's consumers and the broader society, while by design **decoupling the growth
strategy** from Unilever's environmental footprint.

2. Unilever is determined to **go beyond incremental
action and make public commitments** that would
stretch and challenge their capacity.

3. Unilever realized that they might fail but knew the effort would nonetheless change the entire mindset of

the business. Social disclosure matters as much as financial disclosure. This mind-shift creates more social response capitalism with less waste of time, personnel, and money.

4. There is an ambitious global bar stated here, yet there is also a touch of humility.

These four elements you need to see as part of a mosaic.

AMBITIOUS GOAL #1:
IMPROVE HEALTH AND WELL-BEING
FOR >1 BILLION PEOPLE

AMBITIOUS GOAL #2:
REDUCE ENVIRONMENTAL IMPACT BY HALF
(ON ALL MEASURES AND IN PUBLIC)

- Social brand: "decoupling growth."

- Social mantra: cutting impacts in half requires behavioral change, yet Unilever pledges massive change through 2050.

As they commit to reducing impact on the atmosphere, oceans, and land, the Unilever sustainable Living Plan reveals their measurable public pledges.

AMBITIOUS GOAL #3:
ENHANCE LIVELIHOODS FOR MILLIONS

This is standard "declare and defend" corporate thinking, with a new emphasis on "fair compensation."

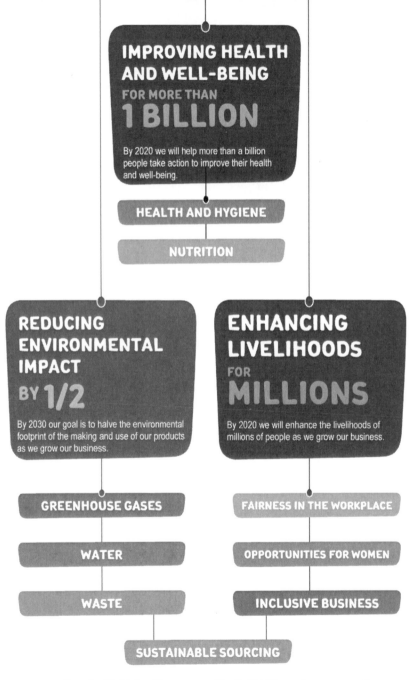

Sustainable Living Plan recreated by Debbi Wraga from www.unilever.com

THE "MAGIC CUBE:" METRICS AND CODES THAT ALLOW "DOING MORE WITH LESS"

Unilever has a special training facility in the United Kingdom, known as Four Acres, for their senior leaders and employees. From 2010 to 2020, at a time when a number of organizations were closing their learning centers, Unilever opened a second Four Acres in Singapore with a €50 million investment in learning and development. Some of these slides come from that curriculum. But how it all makes sense is through what they call "The Magic Cube." This cube can be thought of as their core decision tool. From the Unilever Code: "Codifying the business case is crucial: Otherwise, we are relying on people's belief systems, and that's not how a big corporation will make major long-term decisions and drive real change. Real, lasting change relies on the corporation making sustainability intrinsic to the business itself." It must be sustainable as a business proposition and answer social needs.

Unilever focused on four simple metrics (this alone enables the magic of doing more with less):

1. **More Growth**

2. **Less Risk**

3. **More Trust**

4. **Lower Costs**

Unilever captures this "Magic Cube" better than its peers; however, we also note the emphasis on growth rather than doing more with less.

The Magic Cube: Visually

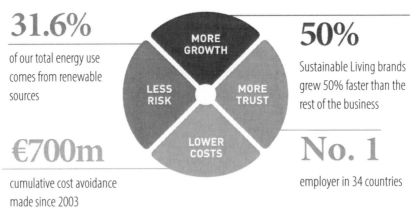

SUSTAINABILITY DRIVING VALUE

31.6%

of our total energy use comes from renewable sources

€700m

cumulative cost avoidance made since 2003

MORE GROWTH

LESS RISK

MORE TRUST

LOWER COSTS

50%

Sustainable Living brands grew 50% faster than the rest of the business

No. 1

employer in 34 countries

Over the next decades people might write entire books on the brilliance of this cube. As a place to start, see Andrew Winston's new book, written with former Unilever CEO Paul Polman, *Net Positive: How Courageous Companies Thrive by Giving More Than They Take.*

This is what I meant earlier by talking about authenticity of approach. The firm admits that only big business can be strong enough to help in certain regions of the world. They also refuse to get "stupid" on excessive things like becoming "anti-growth." In a competitive world, they believe their form of social response capitalism should grow, as others shrink. They would rather have their brand stand tall in the 190 countries than to be caught lying through deceptive PR.

I find this the opposite of being corporate-stupid. That is why it pays now to watch their "internal" thinking out loud in what follows.

Dispensing with Quarterly Reporting

Unilever was one of the first to claim that "big business" can be divided into those with a clear vision of **how their**

business provides value to society, and those that focus on short-term shareholder value. They stated consistently and repeatedly these principles in all nations:

- You cannot focus on driving short-term investor returns while fulfilling a higher corporate purpose.

- Most Unilever employees do not want to work under the old forms of capitalism.

Because of this, upon being named CEO of Unilever in 2009, Paul Polman eventually dispensed with quarterly reporting.

For Unilever, it's all about their social identity and their top brands. Their top 30–35 brands represent 80% of their annual turnover. "This is our North Star: we cannot achieve our purpose if those 30–35 are not operating as Sustainable Living Brands."

A brand's purpose is to give back to society when it can, and to be on a journey to be made in a more sustainable way: less packaging, easier to recycle, etc.

There is a strong and growing trend for consumers choosing brands that give something back: "Consumers will make decisions for you if you don't listen."

Anything the corporation does needs to be additive to Unilever brands; the real power of their customer relationship sits with those brands:

- Unilever is fundamentally about social amplification; a set of social issues like diversity and inclusion, energy competitiveness, and brand recognition.

UNILEVER STATES THAT SOCIETY HAS ALREADY
CHANGED AND WANTS COMPETITIVE FRUGALITY

Unilever believes Society has already changed. I cannot tell you enough about how significant this acknowledgment has become, the acknowledgment that society has already changed its values regarding consumption, climate change, and the need for open organizations and governments. Subscribe to any of the Unilever hashtags on social media and you will see these themes stated clearly, globally, and consistently in many languages and locations. Over half of all global consumers want to purchase more sustainable products. "This trend is even stronger in developing markets," says Rebecca Marmot, Unilever's Chief Sustainability Officer, "as they live with problems in a much more visible way." We benchmark Marmot in one of our ongoing company workshops with 33 global firms before her like bp, Caterpillar, and Trane.

This is the key point in terms of the historic vantage of this book, meant for the years 2022 through 2050: sustainability as a social need is already mainstream. Study these global numbers seen by Unilever:

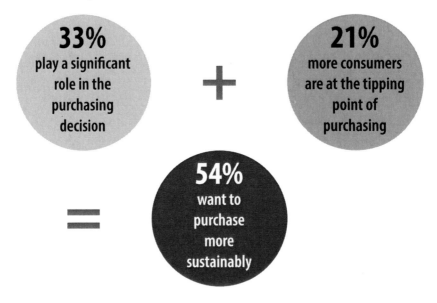

33% play a significant role in the purchasing decision

+

21% more consumers are at the tipping point of purchasing

=

54% want to purchase more sustainably

For more information on this research, please see the Unilever *Making Purpose Pay* PDF.[26]

See also www.DoingMoreWithLessBook.com for a diverse range of case examples, workshops, and lessons.

Unilever: Partnerships for the Goals

Unilever succeeds in finding like-minded, progressive businesses and organizations that share the same goals and have complementary skills, funding, and connections.

Everyone wants solutions, governments included. If people see a critical mass of the business community and other stakeholders, that makes an enormous difference.

Source: 2017 GlobeScan interview with Sue Garrard, then SVP of Sustainable Business & Communications at Unilever.[27]

Unilever has launched a **€1 billion Climate & Nature Fund** (over the next 10 years). This builds on work over the last 15 years that...

- Reduced GHG emissions in dairy (Ben & Jerry's);

- Helped Native Americans access energy;

- Grew food sustainably, from cultivation through delivery to consumers;

- Committed to **Net Zero by 2039**;

- Resolved to work more efficiently with all partners to drive GHG reductions;

---

26 https://www.unilever.com/Images/making-purpose-pay-inspiring-sustainable-living_tcm244-506468_en.pdf

27 https://globescan.com/2017/06/28/webinar-recap-the-2017-sustainability-leaders-survey/

- Sought to know the carbon footprint of every item they sell, with the goal being to coordinate and standardize data collection; and

- Looked at advocacy work they could do with governments.

THE GENIUS AT THE GIANT NEXT DOOR

Keeping the purpose of this book in mind, we need to say that Unilever embodies the notions of competitive frugality in all they do. This case study on Social Response Capitalism suggests Altruism in and of itself won't drive the change needed in a world of more than 7 billion people; food/land/product insights will.

What will drive the change is a clear sense of how this works within the DNA of your business.

In other words, social response capitalism is the train, and everyone on the Unilever train knows they are providing social value, not just products. You can feel the power in this change, which blasts through the current markets like a high-speed train.

You also see from Unilever their participation in two of the biggest challenges of our times: how they are transforming their energy mix to be a responsive agent in this age of climate change and climate immediacy. They started that journey as far back as 2009, when they decided they would not compete on quarterly financial reports.

THE CONSTANT WAVES OF RESISTANCE

Transformation is difficult. The greatest transformation magnifiers are select people. That is why Unilever also participates in the social cohesion efforts of supporting voting, resisting the wrong-headed ads rampant in Facebook that generate social hate and social prejudice.

What makes someone a brilliant deputy at Unilever—and at the firms modeling the same social trends—includes the desire to promote the products and aims that prove indispensable repeatedly, without much prompting. They display internally refined standards, which they deploy across the staff in a continuous visibility. These standards embody the goals of the top leaders. These brilliant deputies do more than add immediate value to the campaign. They communicate pattern, strategy, consistency, and value. They optimize the brave sanctions and social impacts of their corporate teams, as we observed in the Unilever case study.

Clearly the executives running Unilever are bold, audacious, competitive people, who know social trends that matter and the cognitive sciences. They are not content with being followers. These Unilever executives live in society and in the cognitive sciences chasing the nature of their firm in response to many social inputs.

I have been a student of many different firms in my 40 years as a management consultant, and overall, I chose to tell you about Unilever for the purpose of reinforcing the principles outlined in the first fundamental chapters of this book.

They are one of the most honest firms when it comes to the limits of the Earth, the preferences of human behavior, and the need to compete on doing more with less.

SOME WORKING CONCLUSIONS
REGARDING SOCIAL FOCUS

You can sum up Unilever principles in a first-person way, as if spoken directly by Ben Franklin in modern phrasing: **"Sustainability is about the 'social impact.'** Even on environmental aspects, the human dimension is what is truly meaningful. We found constantly that a pure environmental focus makes even our keenest people glaze over. **Focus on better planet, less inequality, better standards of living.** Concentrate on 'What problem are we trying to solve?' This brings you back to *focus* and impact. **Make it emotional, and embed it in social preference, not just current market force.** Focus and impact are social response terms and lens."

YOUR COGNITIVE ACTIONS

Even so, large and impactful firms like Unilever cannot answer all of our social needs alone. They must help in the process of greening all other firms. Bringing all this back to *your* life, let's look at the great work of a single life, the work of Bill Novelli.

UNILEVER TO WILLIAM NOVELLI:
FROM A LARGE FIRM TO ONE CHANGE AGENT

William Novelli was a vital part of our bp transformation team these last years. Novelli started his career at Unilever, and then formed Porter Novelli, a high-impact advisory, and then became the CEO of the world's largest non-profit, the American Association for Retired Persons (AARP). Here is the essence of what Novelli added to our process of accelerating change through doing more with less.

With this humble acknowledgment that no single firm—no matter how large in its global impact—can do it alone, we now turn our attention to the book by William Novelli, *Good Business: The Talk, Fight, Win Way to Change the World*, and his practice, so you can see how social response capitalism involves social action. All of this that follows is directly from the Novelli package of work done at the Georgetown center he runs.

CORPORATE SOCIAL IMPACT: EARNING TRUST THROUGH SOCIAL ACTION

Experience shows that corporations can overcome major social and environmental challenges (partly through coalitions and partnerships, often with "strange bedfellows" to break the mold).

Photo courtesy of: ESB Professional | Shutterstock

What follows outlines a few summary actions William Novelli has led as summed up in his classic *Good Business*:

- **Youth Advocates:** bp can engage with young activists in its global transformation. Kids want climate action. If convinced of bp's authenticity, they can be partners for change.

- **Conservation Organizations:** Volunteers cleaning oil from sea birds was a grim image from the 2015 Gulf of Mexico oil spill. Now, in this new era, bp can become a conservation champion. (Conservation Nation, a new NGO in North America, is a good example.)

- **Physicians and Allied Health Professionals:** The Medical Society Consortium on Climate & Health is an alliance of 30+ U.S. physician groups (e.g., American Medical Association, family physicians, pediatricians) with European counterparts. The Consortium advocates for climate action at national, state, and local levels. Alignment with this prestigious group is a major opportunity.

IN A NUTSHELL: FURTHER EXAMPLES OF SOCIAL PROGRESS ACHIEVED THROUGH SOCIAL ACTION

You are now ready to study the web pages on **Bill Novelli**[28] and *Georgetown University Business for Impact.*[29]

- **CARE International**[30]: Coordinate 16 developed-country NGOs in network to serve 40 low-income coun-

---

28 See https://www.billnovelli.com/

29 See https://businessforimpact.georgetown.edu/

30 See https://www.care-international.org/

tries in agriculture, economic development, women's empowerment, and disaster response.

- **Tobacco Wars:** Negotiate with industry, achieve legislation, drive down youth and adult smoking in U.S. and in low/middle-income countries.

- **Pharma Industry and Medicare:** Engage with companies, achieve legislation enabling seniors to afford prescription drugs.

- **Divided We Fail:** Forge a "strange bedfellows" coalition (large and small companies, trade union, major consumer group) to advocate for health care reform.

- **Philips**[31]**:** Assist worldwide tech company on strategies for healthful aging and public lighting in megacities.

- **VF Corporation**[32]**:** Serve on responsible sourcing advisory committee for VF and its brands (e.g., Timberland, The North Face, Vans) and their contract employees in Asia, Latin America, and Africa.

- **AB-InBev**[33]**:** Assess the company's global responsible-drinking initiatives, present and publish findings and recommendations.

- **Niger Delta Partnership Initiative Foundation**[34]**:** Advise Chevron on its economic development program in Nigeria and publish results.

---

31   See https://www.usa.philips.com/

32   See https://www.vfc.com/

33   See https://www.ab-inbev.com/

34   See https://ndpifoundation.org/

- **Portion Balance Coalition**[35]: Build and lead this alliance of 35+ food and beverage companies (e.g., Unilever, Nestle, PepsiCo), nonprofits, government, and academics to combat obesity.

Overall, the career of William Novelli shows that when a company competes openly and across sustained periods of time regarding shared social needs, they win a bigger place in the consumer's habits and buying patterns. Buyers want social good, not simply convenience. That is what Unilever does. This is what remains for you in the rest of the century.

The point of this finale and coda on the book and life work of William Novelli is simple: when faced with the massive amount of change before us, a person, a leader, and a leadership team need new tools to monitor and to influence social response capitalism. You can think of this as having a career where you help firms bring the outside world's changes more reliably inside the corporate mansion.

This is what Novelli, Bruce Mau, Gordon Lambert, and a host of others have taught me.

---

35 See https://portionbalance.org/

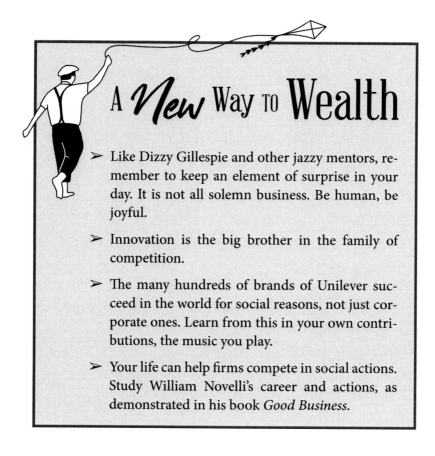

A *New* Way to Wealth

➤ Like Dizzy Gillespie and other jazzy mentors, remember to keep an element of surprise in your day. It is not all solemn business. Be human, be joyful.

➤ Innovation is the big brother in the family of competition.

➤ The many hundreds of brands of Unilever succeed in the world for social reasons, not just corporate ones. Learn from this in your own contributions, the music you play.

➤ Your life can help firms compete in social actions. Study William Novelli's career and actions, as demonstrated in his book *Good Business*.

CHAPTER 6

❧

AN IDLER IN THE CITY: CAPITALISM IS WHERE WE LIVE

"When you have bought one fine thing, you must buy ten more, that your appearance may be all of a piece; but Poor Dick says, 'It is easier to suppress the first desire than to satisfy all that follow it.' And it is as truly folly for the poor to ape the rich, as for the frog to swell, in order to equal the ox."

—Ben Franklin, *The Way to Wealth*

The last ten years (2012–2022) have forced many to focus on a heightened efficiencies of cities, from flood control to clean-energy matters. Many politicians and corporate executives know that capitalism and the fate of megacities are the same fabric fishing out the profitable patterns, as this fabric is key.

A survey of the key megacities of the world—from Athens to Paris and Istanbul to Tokyo—proves the need for new forms of leadership in a world constrained by carbon, capital, and the very nature of capitalism. As waters rise near Manhattan and our most ancient coastal megacities, new forms of competition must emerge and thrive. As we near our shared future, we must humanize more and agitate differences less. It takes an idler-in-the city worldview to see this range of opportunity. By traveling, I have set myself free of naïve and incomplete regional beliefs. My self-esteem is now global. The family of man requires it.

You need to pause, be mindful, celebrate doing more with less to understand this spinning new world of jet and internet immediacy.

Looking Back—and Looking Ahead

In 1976, I ended my first book by saying, "I am looking forward to looking back, because the inaccessibility of any future blinds us in this freshness." At 66, I am glad I wrote that in '76!

When I turned 40, I decided to adopt an open, fun-loving—you might say Whitmanesque—attitude toward business travel. Global travel had become so mean, and so severe (owing to the checks and indignities we have built into travel to deter terrorism), that I had to "put on my patience cap," if you will, and add an extra day a week at each end, to visit the cities before and after I worked in them. This updated chapter grows out of those idle days away from home. I became an "idler" in the great cities.

Photo courtesy of: SPI | Getty Images

Over the past two decades, I have visited over 40 of the top 100 megacities of this world. Each had a marvelously different feel, an inherent personality. Some were warm and exciting, others troubling and suffocating. Yet they also share some common traits. First, they are *growing*. Ninety percent of the future urban increase is expected to take place in Asia and Africa, according to *World Population History*.[36] Second, they are being shaped by a set of fierce and swift social and corporate forces in distinct ways that are often overlooked, or simply ignored.

Why does Athens feel so appealing, like a Paris or a London, while Istanbul and Tokyo feel so large and oppressively overwhelming? And what challenges you when you hit the great sprawls of poverty known as Shanghai, São Paulo, and Mumbai? What unseen forces are controlling and reshaping these cities: local or federal governments, well-financed NGOs like the Gates Foundation, the global press? What provides the engine of their sustained growth? The answers are clear, if you experience your travel at a pace much slower than a rock and roll tour. (I do not pretend to fully answer these book-length questions in an essay of this sort.)

After envisioning the trends in these megacities, you may see a gentle and modest suggestion that this new century will prove different—and luckier—than what anyone supposed. It is my prayer for your children's children that this observation moves globally, not selectively.

SURPRISE, SURPRISE: SOLUTIONS IN COMPETITIVE FRUGALITY

The great and lasting megacities like Athens, Paris, New York, London, Sidney, and Calgary have evolved through the relentless competition for higher and higher efficien-

---

36 https://worldpopulationhistory.org/

cies of labor, resources, and capital that is embodied in global capitalism.

These cities are open to change, to diversity, to inputs from afar. They compete on the edge, where the demand for quality, price, style, and social response unite. For example, they aspire to host the Olympics, and festivals both musical and athletic. One can find them on the map of the great rock 'n' roll tours. And most significantly, they are all teeming with the logic of advanced capitalism, from the multi-speed world of Asia to the mature economies of Europe and North America. Surprise, surprise—the competitive and the frugal thrive in these cities.

Of course, no city is perfect. Racist, exclusionist, and stupid people do resist these changes. It was not so long ago that the suburbs of Paris erupted in riots. London is choking with automobiles. Athens alone holds half the population of the 6,000 Greek islands. But in general, the great cities have embraced globalization in a more intelligent way than the rest; they are going global and going greener at the same time. The experience at FedEx, Microsoft, IBM, Trane, bp, and Unilever confirm this to me.

This collective intelligence about fair competition seems to be based upon the history of populations rather than on religious or cultural beliefs; it is a collective intelligence based on physical facts, if you will. In those megacities that are suffering, it strikes me now that this "group intelligence" about the need to do more with less is still being matured.

There is a good deal of stupidity to erase, along with a fair amount of self-delusion and denial of the realities before all of us. Studying reform in megacities can help erase society stupidity.

Competitive frugality threatens to change those repressive regimes. Over time I predict historians will call the eventual changes the beginning of "the rules of a golden age."

If capitalism continues to uproot repressive regimes as noted in the last four decades, many believe a more compassionate world can re-evolve. Of course, it is naïve to suggest this is a simple linear path. Battles will be fought viciously, yet those left standing will have the principles of this book in their behaviors and policies.

MEGA-COMPANIES SCULPTING MEGACITIES

As every region of the world begins to encounter severe carbon and capital constraints, how are these large megacities—and the mega-companies that they house (companies like HP, GE, ExxonMobil, Shell, and Google)—addressing our urban needs? Are the megacities mobilizing a response to poverty and disease, to crowding and mobility? Are they rebalancing humanity's needs for money, people, and rules?

The best megacities are embracing more public transport and are learning to do more with less. They are preparing for an overpopulated, capital- and carbon-constrained world.

Aware of the threat of rising waters caused by excess carbon in our atmosphere, a number of great cities have already begun climate-change mitigation projects. You might even think of the $15 billion, 245-mile water-control system surrounding the "new" New Orleans as a climate-change mitigation project.

The same goes for the plans underway in Venice, Italy. Firms like AECOM, CH2MHill, Jacobs Engineering, and Arcadis have made billions in those cities by cleaning up past mistakes and building back a better core urban infrastructure.

This is the good news: change toward frugality often occurs outside of federal policy after WWII. I think of these
changes as being based on the higher facts of physical history.[37]

You can cut to the essence of this question about the great
lag of policy by asking the question about "sustainability" in
reverse. You might ask, "Do the 600 largest companies situate
their goods and their talent in the center of these megacities?"
The answer is usually a resounding "No!"

They buy space in suburban Naperville, not in downtown
Chicago. You find HP outside of Heathrow Airport, not in
downtown London. You find Agrium, the world's largest fer-
tilizer firm, outside of downtown Calgary, near a supermarket
and a movie theater in a residential neighborhood. Many of
these giants are clients of my firm, the AHC Group, so I get to
visit their offices, often making 40- to 80-minute commutes
from the airport. It is a capitalist's logic.

Among the 600 largest firms in the world, the pattern is
now almost a commonplace fact. Corporate giants—from
Toyota, Google, and HP to ExxonMobil, Shell, and Walmart—

---

37 But there remains plenty of "policy smoke" and public debate, which
obscures the best plans and prevents these laboratories of innovation from
reaching the rest of the world's coasts. The question of why most federally
elected officials, from President Obama to his Asian equivalents, are ignoring
the higher fact of climate preparation is way beyond me. Perhaps it is because
most governments, at the national security level, are primarily financed by
oil money. If you map the needs of megacities for oil (whether Istanbul, Athens, Paris, Mexico City, Delhi, Shanghai, or Karachi), you rapidly see that
national oil companies in China, Brazil, the Latin oil states, and the Middle
Eastern oil states all employ private multinationals to develop and to exploit
their reserves. I predict a great rebalance by 2025. While total oil production
has declined 4.5 percent annually over the last three years, the push for un-
conventional oil is grossly needed. The reserves may be nationally held (one
number shows that 81% of our global reserves are nationally held), but the
resultant cities and supplying corporations are very much private. Our need
for energy, food, and shelter will redefine our rules so they march more rapidly toward frugality.

know how to pick cheaper, more frugal, and better locations, extending the center city into a megacity and drawing talent, resources, and innovation after them. This has had many positives, and one big negative. Urban sprawl and long commutes result in an excess of driving, which helps fuel climate change. How can we outsmart this? Many have asked if this is a net good. I ask: How can we call this anything but the relentless logic of social response capitalism?

I believe that the changes in this new century boil down to two related things: globalization in more efficient goods and services, and our shared sustainability needs. You see both when you look at our needs in terms of food, transportation, and dwellings in a smaller world. You cannot have one without the other. We need both sustainability and globalization; and getting the best of both resides in competition and frugality.

This is what William Throop, the Provost of Green Mountain College, meant when he said "the global benefit of frugality is that it moves our emphasis from financial capital to social capital." He further refined his claim by noting how frugality enters the city and commerce as "a rich means to buffer individualism by building and maintaining robust social networks."

While many articulate critics lament this cultural development, I see it as the blue sky of hope and resourcefulness amid the clouds of sprawl. To quote Throop again, "The real social dimension in competing on sustainability is that it gives the world a problem-solving disposition." It is the kind of urban encounter that helps humans learn how to develop within themselves the capacity to draw things out of a group, and achieve the wisdom of teams.

You can question whether it is right, or all for the best, but you cannot really question why rising populations and the "corporate race to efficiency" sit together in megacities like a hand in a glove. There is something incredibly rapid and shocking about global consolidation: things grow exponentially overnight. Each week, one large company merges with another; one city merges with its neighbor. We see it happen all the time, but we don't exactly know what it means.

SPLENDID SISTERS

Maybe it is better to think of them as sisters: active and engaged siblings. It is better to think of corporate behavior and the lust for frugality and efficiency in human terms, thus the analogue of sisters. But others approach it in a more indirect way—witness this related tale from a Senator.

In Washington, D.C., I once shared a short elevator ride with a senator from an oil state; he actually had his aide press the "stop" button so that we could continue our quick conversation. As we discussed this global tendency toward consolidation, he said, "Certainly, the seven sisters—the world's largest oil players—must be doing something right to get that big. It couldn't just be their love of debt, their faith in complex technologies, and their thirst to span the globe. They must be doing something right, don't you think?" Knowing how far his tenure and his reach were financed by energy and "the infrastructure," we opened the elevator doors in a state of polite disagreement. Yet his force opened my eyes.

I've been pondering this question for a quarter of a century now, since I have visited most of these oil giants. Of those original seven, only five remain. My firm works for three of them.

And what exactly did the Senator mean by "doing something right"? Right in terms of money? Right in terms of people? Right in terms of the rule of fair competition? Are these developments right for the environment, right for people of all means, right for the profitability of the owners, regardless of the cost to others?

I cannot begin to answer these important questions on equity, but I think you will see that there is something "right" about the hand-in-glove relationship that has emerged between most megacities and capitalism. It goes much deeper than shared fashions.

CORPORATE CULTURE AND MEGACITIES

Consider a few higher facts. Our consulting practice now treats these five higher facts as basic as physics and waves at a seashore:

1. Over seventy of the 100 largest economies in the world are not nations: they are global, earth-spanning corporations like bp and Unilever, often working in over 115 nations.

2. From Copenhagen to Caracas, firms exist in the globe now—not just in nation states. You find global brands and products in all megacities.

3. The 100 largest multinational corporations (MNCs) now control about 33 percent of global foreign assets. These top 100 are household names—like Google, HP, Walmart, Toyota, and Shell. Most children today know these names better than the names of nations or states.

4. Three hundred MNCs now hold at least a third of the world's total assets. This figure I have reconfirmed

several times since publication of my book *World Inc* (2007), and those holdings continue to grow daily.

5. More than half of world trade now occurs within these top multinationals. That number is updated from the trends first reported in *World Inc*. These trends grow parallel with the growth of the megacities.

If we think of global commerce like slices in a shared pizza pie, you can see how many of the slices are already about business-to-business exchange, rather than regional policy questions or the tax and safety concerns of nation-states.

B2B, or business to business, can be more frugal than policy, more competitive and more direct than government work and rules. Think about Google, Walmart, and GE here, and most any of the Fortune 500. This is the way of the world, the way of our flesh and bones. Yet, how many times have you thought about B2B today?

I believe that once we adjust our attitudes to deal with this new frontier—in which corporations, not nation-states, are ascendant—we will find that this new, globalized world can help improve our cars and our homes; our computers and our appliances; our food and our health; and the length, comfort, and satisfaction of our lives.

My theory may be unwanted news in the eyes of sun-drenched farmers or rural intellectuals, but I am talking here about the clear majority of us—no matter our nation, beliefs, or circumstances. **This is about the only higher fact missing from the great old classics I love. For it is a new higher fact, a fact of the new 21st century.** It was not empirically timely before my little life nor yours.

This century is about the logic of capitalism and the logic of megacities: the physical manifestation of a new kind of

21st-century global capitalism that ceaselessly seeks to improve in a swift and severe way.

Is this all for the good? Absolutely not, you know that. But my point is that we need to start with the facts.

The United Nations Millennium Project examined, through nine richly detailed books, how the old forms of industrial capitalism led to over two dozen failed states—from Somalia to spot islands and select Latin states. Nearly a billion and a half of the world's inhabitants live in areas where poverty is on the rise. It would be naïve to say that capitalism has been kind to these places. But my point is that it is blind to stop with that statement.

Corporate globalization is not something new or something in the future that we can plan for or decide upon. It is already here, just as our megacities are already here. It is our understanding of the value shift that is lagging. Virtually no place on earth is shielded from the actions of large multinationals. There are few inhabitants of this globe whose days are not directly shaped by the choices of these firms, from the food we choose to make for dinner to the tools we use to get our jobs done and keep our families safe.

THE TRUTH ABOUT GLOBAL CORPORATIONS

According to the UN, by 2050—a mere 28 years from now—almost three-quarters of the world's population will live in cities. Oil, energy, personal mobility, and the price of goods are the central variables that have made—and will make—rapid urbanization possible.

We already live in a world where, for the first time in human history, most people live in urban mega-clusters. This is also the same world in which most of your water, air, housing, and food have been processed by corporations before you use it. My premise is simple: mega-companies should have mega-responsibilities. This is a fundamental higher fact, like a high-rise in the Middle East or skyscrapers in Manhattan and other megacities.

We should expect more from these corporations who are in charge of so many aspects of our lives. And of this new expectation requires a new kind of social leader.

Photo courtesy of: DoroshinOleg | bigstockphoto.com

Capitalism Today and Tomorrow

I first began thinking about the constraints on carbon, capital, and capitalists in the late 1980s, on a boat ride from Manhattan to Albany sponsored by then-governor Mario Cuomo. Cuomo and his deputy, Stan Lundine, had organized a 50-person thought experiment called New York 2000—a boat ride up the Hudson, during which the 50 participants would debate the legitimate role of government in securing a better New York, from the city itself to the upstate hinterlands.

Most of the folks on the boat were lawyers, executives, or bankers; I was there as a sort of corporate resource expert, as my first two books (published in the 1980s) had helped reshape federal laws around hazardous waste management. As we were passing the citadels of West Point, the governor asked us for our working definitions of altruism. After several attempts at defining why people go beyond the call of duty, David Sive, a Park Avenue attorney and co-founder of the Natural Resources Defense Council, told a story I will never forget.

He had been stationed in the Italian Alps during World War II. Guarding a snowy summit, he was under orders to shoot anyone who came across the valley and didn't know the Allied Forces' code word, which changed nightly.

It was early morning, and a figure approached, barely visible in the blinding whiteout. Reciting his orders to himself, Dave thinks, "Shoot, you fool." But he doesn't shoot. He ignores the orders of his superiors. He decides to resist tradition and his own past practice. The figure turned out to be an Allied soldier who was lost—and therefore didn't know the password.

Dave finished the story by saying, "And you suppose I didn't shoot for some altruistic reason?" He paused so his audience could weigh in. Most people felt he was a hero.

He did not.

He said it wasn't altruism that stopped him. "My loaded gun remained loaded that morning not due to any higher selfless good," he said. "Yes, I saved that nameless Allied soldier from death, not because I knew he was on our side, nor because I somehow sensed he had been lost in the storm for three days."

The pause was palpable. "I did it out of basic fear. I was afraid I would make a mistake."

The candor of his confession has consequences.

In my experience with leaders I have come to trust, they often operate out of basic instincts—from fear to longing to love of competition for its own sake. You can give them all the numbers, explore all the legal nuances, even cascade the dance of consequences before them, but none of it matters as much as what's inside them.

Capitalism is at a crossroads because more and more people who head and support businesses have within them the desire to help make a better world, even if it means they need to kill inherited prejudices. These are the captains of tomorrow, the navigators of the megacity of today.

ELIMINATING SMALL-MINDED PREJUDICE

One of the best ways to eliminate prejudice and other destructive preconceptions is to cut through their waste with frugality. We have often gone to war out of fear, out of a sense of profound differences of belief. There is some proof that regions of the world give up the sword, and put down their weapons, when excess is cut out from their wants.

This cultural openness is the newest element in advanced capitalism. Jefferson and Franklin were right: we achieve the likelihood of peace through commerce, through the efficient encounter of values with others.

Over the last decade, I wanted to update my working knowledge of the principles of this book by writing about contemporaries, not just Jefferson and Franklin. What follows is a visual reminder of the six exemplar lives I spent a decade writing and studying, people like the diplomat Frank Loy; the former bp CEO Steve Percy; the investing wisdom of John Streur and Jack Robinson; the quiet genius of the fashion CEO Eileen Fisher; and the social intelligence of Linda Coady. In each case, I saw the principles of this book enacted in their lives. In short, these biographies are further compelling evidence of the power of doing more with less.

These leaders and people are fiercely competitive, yet I call them civil, frugal, and creative. They, in general, hold their fire—allowing diversity and a sense of the globe, to fill their streets, to populate their megacities.

Going Back to the School of Social Leadership

Certainly, the city of the future needs the engines of capitalism: cars, computers, better manufacturing, and so on. But in addition to more efficient things to address our mobility and efficiency needs, we require a mind-shift to the principles of competitive frugality. Megacities will help make all of us sense a larger purpose and our role in it. By their very nature, they inspire us to dream big and suggest that we can become more. They are the beehive in which we see our honey; they give us our direction and our sense of what we must protect. And the businesses that survive in this challenging new millennium will need to find new and lasting ways to answer key social questions—involving poverty, mobility, and energy diversity—and we need them *now*.

And those that answer best will be the makers of the great cities.

Golden ages are times of peace, creativity, prosperity, and openness all at once. If you dislodge one, you hurt another, as defilement is never an isolated event. You need to become, like Franklin in your great city, a person at once frugal, diplomatic, loyal, and inventive.

Today, Tomorrow, Megacities

There is plenty of room in this world view, and you can create new possibilities for yourself, your firm, and your family in a world both swift and severe.

Whether you are growing up in a rapidly growing economy like Brazil, China, or India, or maturing an approach in the old world of Europe and North America, this book brings you home in our globalized but still not flat world. The new key to your future is to find the right balance between competitiveness and frugality in all of us.

Readers in Australia, Latin America, and Asia understand this need for the arts of competitive frugality almost instinctively. These residents of our world know about the water droughts of Australia, of the poverty of the Latin states, of the fierce competitiveness based on frugality in most of Asia. It is a part of their family and personal culture. They have helped inspire the promise of this book, and I've benefited from their wealth and creativity.

FOR THOSE STILL DOUBTFUL

I admire your reluctance to be persuaded. Yet I am also persistent.

Of course, there will be pockets of industrial and public resistance to this call for competitive frugality. There will be years of political doubt, voiced by talking heads that are mostly accountants and legal experts. And there will be long procedural delays, as the best firms laugh their way to the bank on frugality. There will be periods historians will describe as eras of rampant regional indulgence by consumers, in pursuit of a fading happiness.

But overall, the redemptive force we find is a force as primal as human and natural history.

As the population density in megacities blossoms, I see on the streets and in the headquarters I visit a major new convergence on the challenges of our carbon- and capital-constrained world. This offers new grounds for hope. Perhaps all this talk about positive trends in megacities will prove delusional in some abrupt retreat in history. But I, for sure, do not see that reactionary return to waste likely in my lifetime.

When I wrote my 1990 book *In Search of Environmental Excellence*, there was hardly a ripple of change in the firms in these directions, let alone a sea-change. Today, many of you are ready to answer the call for a new generation of management tools, new principles for life, and more efficient designs that allow us to go global as we go greener.

"We are what we make and do," my grandmother used to say. I see you making better products for a better world, from cars and computers, to your homes and your backyards.

New Grounds for Hope

I see many of you ready to meet the needs of our changing cities and climate, despite political confusion or serious corporate foot-dragging. You seem ready to build net-zero-energy buildings and to create the levees needed to answer rising sea levels in Venice, in New Orleans, and in Washington's precious military corridors. I see many in the technical realms ready to construct large-scale mass transit systems for modern mobility. These are the impelling energies whose intent is to spread frugality in our support systems and thereby protect a civilization.

It is clear that this new kind of capitalism is exactly what is needed in our world's megacities.

The tide may shift rapidly to danger and stark darkness unless we become frugal in time. I see it as a window of great opportunities for all. What I've observed about the relationship between capital and cities is likely to be at the center of a series of serious public choices about doing more with less.

In our swift, severe, and competitive world, I hope a majority of the people that populate these megacities will learn, in time, these historic lessons about competition, frugality, and our shared future. For there is not enough fencing and cement in the world to wall you off from the rest. There is a strong, frontal rudeness to some of these facts, like death itself. It is up to you to either accept this future or be isolated by it.

"Morning has broken," notes the singer formerly known as Cat Stevens. He then sings praise to the voice of the blackbird, and the way each day offers a new world of faith, certain of a new day, a chance to be mindful. I add to this wonder the joys of doing more with less.

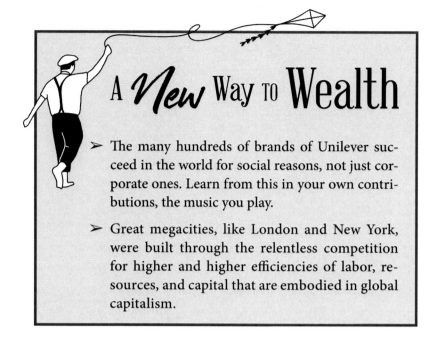

A *New* Way to Wealth

➤ The many hundreds of brands of Unilever succeed in the world for social reasons, not just corporate ones. Learn from this in your own contributions, the music you play.

➤ Great megacities, like London and New York, were built through the relentless competition for higher and higher efficiencies of labor, resources, and capital that are embodied in global capitalism.

Part 3:

NEAR THE FUTURE

- Recurrent themes: Thriving in an age of carbon and capital constraints.

- The power is doing more with less.

- Empower the near future by helping children be Ben Franklin all over again.

PROLOGUE

⁂

DOING MORE WITH LESS IN SONG

BY STEVE GILLETTE

We know that music enriches our lives, and we give ourselves over to its magic; at least when it's performed by our heroes of the pop charts, or the masters of the classics. But often we say to ourselves, "Could I ever do that? Of course not. That's for the talented ones, the gifted few who have the magic. The ones who've shown promise from childhood and have been nurtured and coached until they can bring the instrument or the voice to life." It's something we can't imagine doing ourselves.

But that doesn't mean we can't be part of this magical world. While I do respect the gifts that talented people exhibit, and the work they have done to reach the level of perfection that enchants us, I am happy to tag along and do what I can with what I have to bring to it. Doing more with less, so to speak.

As a songwriter, I can sing my own songs for anybody who will listen, but I also have the opportunity to have someone else sing my songs, someone who has the wherewithal to sell a million records and perform for an audience larger than all the people I might reach with my own voice in a lifetime. I've been fortunate to hear my songs sung by many of the celebrated voices of my generation.

While we might aspire to great wealth and fame, that doesn't often come without a concerted campaign of some kind. You might have a terrific soup recipe, but the chance of garnering room on the shelves of every supermarket in the land might require the coordinated efforts of thousands of corporate minions, while all you really desire is one good bowl of soup. With a good song, you can have both.

So, what's keeping us from speaking directly to the hopes and dreams of the whole world? Nothing at all, really. I can't say that I consciously set out to imprint my notes and words on a hundred million records (or CDs, cassettes, downloads, streams, or what have you). I just followed my bliss, as they say. That meant learning a lot of the popular tunes, picking up pointers and tricks, music theory when I was ready for it, but never losing touch with the backbeat of enchantment that music has always held.

By the time we're nine years old, we've heard it all. We can whistle just about everything ever written. Try this experiment: sing "Twinkle, Twinkle, Little Star."

If that feels silly, then you have a little sense of the resistance you'll learn to overcome, whether it be fear of failure, fear of being caught wasting precious time, anxiety over your vocal performance, or "I can't carry a tune in a bucket." There are hundreds of voices of inhibition, and we've heard them all. Now we'll ignore them and have some fun.

So come on, sing "Twinkle, Twinkle, Little Star." Just the first two phrases. Experiment a little with the key, higher or lower, until it's comfortably in your range. Now if you're sure nobody is listening, let yourself get into the performance of it, big voice, or conspiratorial, or joyful. Try to see how much you can identify with the simple lyric, and feel where you would want it to go to be truly expressive of your own personal view of the cosmos.

Then do this for me. When you come down to that last note on the word "are" at the end of the second phrase, stay on that note and then sing, "and I say to myself"; and then, with just a little adjustment of the melody, "what a wonderful world." When I discovered the similarity between that huge hit song and the simple child's tune, it was empowering. It said to me, "Yeah, I can do that." There's nothing new under the sun, just new arrangements of old elements.

There's a reason we say that we "play" music, and we can't let that be discounted. Out of the play comes the fun, and the enjoyment that bonds us to the creation of a song that we care about. Others will care about it too if we do the work, but the play is how we will be guided in that work.

Lucky is the child who has a piano to reach up and make sticky with his curious fingers, but even the cheapest drug-store keyboard or toy store xylophone can connect us with the notes on the page, or the copyright form when it's time for that. Even if we can't tell a tuplet from a semiquaver, we can hum our tune into a smart phone. (Some of those phones can even tell you if they've heard that tune before.)

The important thing is that nothing gets in the way of the fun, like a three-year-old with finger paints who is gleefully splattering the walls. It's our heartfelt best out there on our sleeve. We've taken care to make it presentable, but always have honored where it came from in the process.

This "play-work" is the work of the songwriter, as it is of the painter and the playwright and the poet. It's a visit to the great library of the mind, not always available to us in our goal-oriented, hunting-gathering, day-to-day struggle, but essential in our dialog with the soul.

It's often called "creative visualization," and it's available to us always. But it's funny how it shows up when we're doing the dishes, or riding on a bus, or not doing the thing that we're being paid to do. Funny also that the paycheck from a song that might come to us in a moment of play can be the equal of a lifetime of work at a "real" job.

The two are not in conflict: the one provides for the other, and together they sustain us. The thing I would stress, if I haven't done so already, is that it is the dialog with the ear and the heart that is where the gift is to be found. In a movie filled with memorable lines, I remember Lauren Bacall saying to Humphrey Bogart, "Just whistle."

—Steve Gillette
August 2021

CHAPTER 7

❧

THE WONDER OF CHILDREN:
THEIR WORLD OF TOMORROW

"Thus, the old gentleman ended his harangue. The people heard it, and approved the doctrine, and immediately practiced the contrary, just as if it had been a common sermon; for the auction opened, and they began to buy extravagantly. However, I resolved to be the better for the echo of it; and though I had at first determined to buy stuff for a new coat, I went away, resolved to wear my old one a little longer. Reader, if thou wilt do the same, thy profit will be as great as mine. I am, as ever, thine to serve thee."

—Ben Franklin, *The Way to Wealth*

Franklin's admonitions are special. Yes, keep your old coat on, my friends, and prepare for many to ignore the warnings before us. This could make some of our shared future quite chilling.

I consider Franklin one of my friends for several reasons. While so many squander value, he compounded it for me. His sharp attacks at waste, the ways he outmaneuvered the average knucklehead, and his summons for us to be industrious and frugal in our future resonates in me like a Beethoven symphony. As noted by Richard Restak, a Clinical Professor of Neurology at George Washington Hospital School of Medicine and Health Sciences (and other cognitive scientists thinking along the same lines), "Creativity is based on three thinking patterns: verbal language, in which unwarranted assumptions can trip us up; music and math, which require the understanding of fundamentals; and visual thinking, which is often key to the creative by enabling us to envision and manipulate information."

Even after centuries, Franklin's sportive seriousness sounds almost like Restak's definition of creativity above. He is clever. He is honest. He is open. He knows people will be people, girls will be girls, boys will be boys, yet he embraced changing rules with grace and wit as he matured. And he always remembered, in a primal way, that money will shine its truths onto people, as history changes. Some will be swamped by money (whether in the owning of it or in the pursuit of it), while others can be lifted by it. Franklin's words have a higher fidelity to them, like a serious jingle.

But where will the new songs of this century come from? Steve Gillette's reflection on how songwriting relates to doing more with less is profound. It is timely now for you to write some songs, to get what Steve Gillette means about the musicality of songwriting available in our lives. His book on the creative process will give you a leg up in that direction. It is called *Songwriting and the Creative Process: Suggestions and Starting Points for Songwriters.* I highly recommend it to up-and-coming new learners. He wrote for Graham Nash ("Teach Your Children"), Tom Paxton ("The Last Thing on My Mind"), and numerous other performers. And many millions more have listened to his songs, not knowing his name.

In reading Steve Gillette's book, you will come across the essentials of creativity from some of the greatest thinkers on the subject—as Steve developed his songwriting techniques on the shoulders of giants like Joseph Campbell, Gertrude Stein, and Carl Jung, not to mention Rollo May. They helped Steve learn how to access "pure thought" and translated emotive complexities into frugal songs.

The key is to think about the needs of the children of the world as you write your songs, or make your films, or build your organizations. To become a successful leader, one path is to help children become like Ben Franklin all over again. This chapter is meant to have you start a journey of your own in competitive frugality, imagining first the needs of children.

Steve Gillette challenges you, as his listeners, to write your own songs. In having you think through the needs of children, we are having you think about parenting in the near future in this time of climate change.

This chapter is a short photo-essay, with bulleted segmented links to other facts and sources so you can curate your own learning in this area.

I now choose, for several reasons, to present you with a break from normal expository writing, with this image of Bruce Springsteen.

Photo courtesy of:
Ebet Roberts | Getty Images

Like "The Boss," I am far from my childhood, but I feel its lessons of childhood every time I hear a Van Morrison song or a Bruce Springsteen song. Great songwriters show us the vivid links between creativity and scarcity. They do so much with so little.

This relates to childhood in a thousand ways. I tried to leave many naked gaps in this chapter so you can fill in the blanks. As you read on, why not play the early works of The Boss?

- Springsteen is synonymous with the working class.
- He embodies the blue-collar worker, doggedly trying to make ends meet.
- I feel that my ideas of social wealth were achievable in my life, helping me form the Creative Force Foundation Inc public charity to give back, because I retained a "working class" sensibility despite my decades of work.
- This means that I tried to resist becoming an elite, a dignified puppet. I remained defiant in my need to keep things simple and working class again and again, as in the life of Pat Mahoney.
- "Streets of Philadelphia" was written to accompany the film *Philadelphia*, which gave audiences a very rare and sobering look into the life of a man diagnosed with HIV/AIDS. The song inspired much controversy, as homosexuality and AIDS were not widely accepted as topics of discussion, let alone as topics of rock songs.
- An early proponent of diversity and human rights, Springsteen starred in a social media campaign in 2012 that promoted same-sex marriage in several states. He has demonstrated his support for gay rights in interviews, in letters posted on his website, and during his performances at campaign rallies for both of Barack Obama's presidential runs.

- Being sensitive to the plights of the underserved, even when at the heights of a Bruce Springsteen, takes artful talents demonstrated as valuable in this book.

We are verbal creatures, and our brains thrive on song and film. Think through your songs for the near future, visualizing solutions for children.

Now we are ready to contemplate the global plights of children, in the context of scarcity; and to celebrate the clever, creative ways survivors mature. For in figuring out how to do so much with so little, children have taught me that skill throughout my life. And they give you these truths without a legal or accounting bill!

Thinking about the unfortunate in a song like "Streets of Philadelphia," you can feel the need to also think about children as an imperative to do more with less. Here are some opening facts:

Nearly half of Argentine children live in poverty, according to a 2020 Catholic University of Argentina (UCA) study.[38]

- 48.1% of children in urban Argentina live in a home that doesn't have an average income necessary to reach the Canasta Básica Total (or CBT, the income amount needed to rise above the poverty line), which is around 15,135 Argentine pesos a month (equivalent to US$518).

- 10% live in severe poverty, in households where the income doesn't exceed the Canasta Básica Alimentaria of 6,189 pesos (US$212 dollars).

- 30% live in houses that are labeled as unsafe due to the materials used in their construction.

- 19% have insufficient access to education (2017).

- 10% lack sufficient food.

- 23.3% lack basic health care.

- 15% lack access to technology.

- 17% find themselves in a vulnerable situation emotionally or intellectually in the first three years of life.

- 65% experience some form of deficiency, representing 8.2 million children throughout the country.

The miracle of youth is its openness to learn. Children need to know higher facts; they smile when they hear reliable guiding principles.

---

38 See: https://www.nbcnews.com/news/latino/argentina-nearly-half-poverty-coronavirus-deepens-economic-crisis-n1241704

Photo courtesy of: Paola Rodriguez | Partners in Health

CHILDREN ROCK

My points across the beginning two thirds of this book are now more applied than ever. Facing the fact that nearly half of the children of Argentina live in poverty, and that the prior numbers regarding Africa and children in general appear overwhelming, it is important to trust the principles and the promise in this book.

Look at children's smiles. They know what to expect only across time. Let's give them a chance.

For a boy in rural Mexico, hearing aids offer a new sense of freedom.[39]

- CES recognized a gap in care for rural areas and created a referral program to link local health centers and hospitals, doing more with less.

---

[39] See: https://www.pih.org/article/boy-rural-mexico-hearing-aids-offer-new-sense-freedom

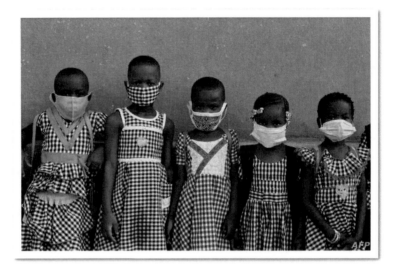

Photo courtesy of: Issouf Sanogo | Getty Images

CHILDREN SING THROUGH MASKS

Children wearing face masks gather outside their class-room at a school in Abidjan, Ivory Coast, May 25, 2020.[40]

- "School closures are potentially exacerbating risks of teenage pregnancies, of violence against children, of substance abuse, of anxiety, loneliness and isolation."

- Only a quarter of schools in Sub-Saharan Africa have basic hygiene services; just 44% have safe drinking water; and only 47% have basic sanitation services.

- The children will walk miles every day to school and will learn to social distance and wear masks.

---

40 See: https://www.voanews.com/a/africa_africa-health-officials-call-children-return-school/6194728.html

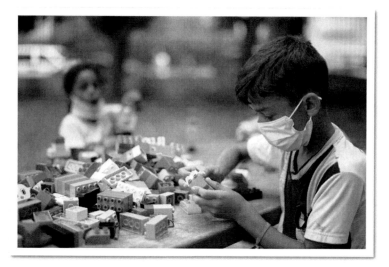

Photo courtesy of: Choufany | UNICEF

CHILDREN TEACH PARENTS HOW TO SURVIVE

Increased support vital to help children affected by Beirut explosions back to school, one month after devastating explosions.[41]

- At least 163 public and private schools were damaged by the explosions—impacting. over 70,000 students and 7,600 teachers.

- 600,000 children could be suffering negative short-term and long-term psychological impacts.

- The challenges of learning from home during Covid-19 for children grows larger when many face damage or destruction.

- UNICEF has been distributing aid to as many as possible, delivering 18 shipments of critical humanitarian supplies, totaling 67 tons, in addition to local procurement of emergency supplies.

---

41 See: https://www.unicef.org/press-releases/increased-support-vital-help-children-affected-beirut-explosions-back-school-one

You may notice that only a few of the children profiled in these hyperlinked stories are "white." It is worth thinking through what is the moral obligation of whites and the wealthy to address these mounting social issues. What is the fixed ratio between your own wealth and your generosity to those in need?

REFLECTION RELATING TO PERSONAL FREEDOM

Today we live in a world where a number of people do not know the relationship between personal freedom and social responsibility. We must fight to realign money, people, and rates to better respect the social obligations in wealth and its freedom.

Watch the children who learn this vital link early in life. They are our best grounds for hope.

By contrast, the most vivid anti-examples are those that have easy, cost-free access to Covid-19 vaccinations, yet mistakenly think that that access, not to mention the government's encouragements to "take the shot," are violations of their personal freedom.

Think about safety belts in cars. Think about the care your child received when first birthed in a hospital, and the preventive measures your pediatrician took on behalf of your child while you rested and recovered from the rigors of childbirth.

Think about what stupidity there is in social history. Stupidity does not mean unintelligent or uninformed positions. Many of those refusing vaccines are well-educated individuals, highly advantaged elites by any measure, who have somehow forgotten that their primary job is to protect children and finance the future.

There is a third powerful force in the world besides science and faith in human nature, and it is best summed up as "stupidity." In the beginning parts of this book, I referred to it as "knucklehead behaviors."

The survival of others is the first thing one learns in military training. In my book *Doing More With Teams*, I wrote about "sharing shoulder strength" as the metaphor of how to deal with the overwhelming issue of other people's needs. Flinging in their faces descriptive adjectives like "delusional," "obstinate," "perverse," and "selfish" is not a sufficient response in this time of carbon and capital constraints. Personal freedom is nothing without survival. Is it any wonder, then, that the "protest song" of these anti-vaxxers—once they find themselves hooked up to a respirator in a hospital ICU—quickly turns into a beggar's opera?

HOW TO TAKE ON THE KNUCKLEHEADS: OUTPLAY THEM

By this I mean you need a little anger, a little animus, a little fire in the belly to take on those that are doing "stupid" things. It is one thing to tolerate the occasional unkindness. It is another to allow actions that prevent social solutions, or that encourage propaganda whose chief aim is to convince people to reject reality. We cannot wall ourselves off from the plight of immigrants, or from the needs of children.

THE FINAL PREDICAMENT: THE FATE OF CHILDREN

When we consider the radiance of children, there is hope. When we consider fiercely the predicament of the children, we need principles.

Transforming society for a cleaner energy future, and as a response to climate change, takes mobilizing the children into lifestyle changes, innovation actions, and supportive partnerships. We need to do the same kind of principled social actions with our medical establishment, with conservation networks, and through international alliances. This cleaning of the firm is not a simple, over-a-few-nights gesture. Instead, look at the 27 nations of Europe and their Fit for 55 plans as the first steps beyond baby steps the world will take.

What I now ask for is a bit more demanding, in my personal life, than those that stay for hours in a state of mindfulness.

Thinking right is a weak sister to acting right. The challenges I face each day in my work and writing require action, not enlightenment.

My staff keeps growing, my client needs become mirrors to some larger social needs, and everyday concerns present themselves as almost brand new. In response, with my wife I have created The Creative Force Foundation Inc to award the best business and society writers in the United States, Africa, Australia, the United Kingdom, and Ireland as a way to acknowledge the value of their contributions.

You are required at the end of each chapter to look back over the action lists provided, and to judge what's right for your actions. Be like William Novelli and Pat Mahoney here. This book is all about how you remain in the game for the future without losing your footing in humanity. And that has as much to do with you and your friends as with me and my principles.

Your Actionable Songs

I believe you need to load new songs into your playlists as described by Steve Gillette in his short piece on songwriting in the Prologue to Part 3. Take them to the gym, and wire them into your family, wherever they gather for feasts and festivities. What you once called your time—your time for yoga, your time for reading, your time for self-discovery—might soon become your entire day. Cultural creatives achieve this wholeness, and they often achieve that freedom from fate through frugality and friendship, not excess or constant doing.

Watch an Alison Krauss, for example, master her duets with James Taylor and John Waite. James Taylor co-sings with Mark Knopfler a beautiful and dangerous new-century ballad called "Sailing to Philadelphia." I have listened to this duet about the creators of the Mason-Dixon Line with wide-eyed appreciation. It helped me conceive this chapter.

The song is rich with historic narrative as the two explorers, Jeremiah Dixon and Charlie Mason, both wild and different in their own ways, describe their risky mission to "chart the evening sky." They are making a new America, and they know this new world awaits their decisions. They are taking risks that are required, realigning money, people, and rules by the boundary they draw for their time: the Mason-Dixon Line.

One refrain reflects on the likelihood that what they are compelled to complete might prove fatal. They can feel the weight of an opponent's warring differences nearing them. As they turn into a new bay, they look beyond the current horizon of worry, beyond the bay, to where another day will make clear their mission. There is a very human feeling in this song, this willingness to do what you must, knowing resistance, but knowing another day will tell all.

I find that song, sung in a kind of future perfect tense, a fitting way to experience this chapter. Yes, in works of consequence, it is the next days that matter. As Franklin often noted, each day you dig yourself out of a constrained past puts you closer to a better tomorrow.

Many of the principles of this short book, such as our statements about the art of competitive frugality, will become more real over time. As we turn the corners into our shared tomorrows, these principles will unfold with more force and certainty. Can you feel that now in your bones?

Early adopters of these principles, from Marcus Aurelius to Benjamin Franklin to E.F. Schumacher, saw the need to compete for frugality, sustainability, and new products before the advent of wall-to-wall people. This will need the reinforcing strength of luxury taxes on fourth homes, luxury cars, and luxury boats, plus stricter environmental and financial rules.

What matters now is generations of them, the tidal flow now forming. Prepare your sails, my friends. Find the right tack, with wit. Joy, as manifested in personal and family satisfaction, awaits those that limit debt and compound social value.

The fundamentals of money, people, and rules, although ever changing by dint of politics and the whim of fate, will erect some lasting fixed features of your life. We must master this life of carbon and capital constraints, the way the American frontier families overcame their obstacles and woes.

You can do it. These old, time-tested principles in this book fit us like Franklin's old coat. I stated in part two that Fate Respects Frugality. **The only way home is doing more with less.**

Ending Tale

The future history of competition and frugality will mount with time. When, for example, the eighth billion human is born into this world, or then, the tenth billion, the equations of this book become more accurate in a starker sense of truth.

Social history underscores the bottom lines on climate impacts, industrial pollution, and the better companies over time.

Life for each of us is short, and anguish abounds, but what I know is that you can feel the future in your life through frugality. In addition, it is known that most new corporations fail within five years because of debt, eroding margins from exploiting staff or customers. You cannot make financial capital in the absence of social capital for very long.

Each person added to our vast universe of competition for consumer goods adds a further reason to compete for frugality. I cannot erase the anguish evident in the needs of people on earth, nor erase the pain of poverty, the shanty towns, the bribed officials, the weak leaders of my daughter's profoundly near future. But there is another way to brighten this near future. Europe's 27 nations call it "Fit for 55," package of new directives and regulations of the European Commission with regard to the climate policy of the European Union. These agreements aim to be frugal, innovative, and inclusive and are designed to decrease carbon emissions by 55 percent by 2030, when this book will be a mere nine years old! It is already in the works, with earnest expected results.

It is your future, or it is not. You have the choice before you. You can become fit for competition or prepare to be one of the 95 percent of new firms that will fail by 2030. This is the way of the world, a world of swift and severe right thinking and fidelity of teams.

Writers write to transform their physical bodies into deathless words. But the physics surrounding their short lives remain immutable. These rules of humanity are set in our hearts. We are hardwired for this form of competition.

The principles and physics for frugality are set now before us. These are not really political or ideological decisions, as they are based on physical facts and social norms. **We cannot change them, but we can change ourselves, for the chance to repress the importance of these facts is lessening with each new birth.**

If tomorrow I were to become a translucent body, a mere ghost of my empirical self, the equations for frugality remain. It is your children's fate to compete more passionately, and more honestly, for this prize.

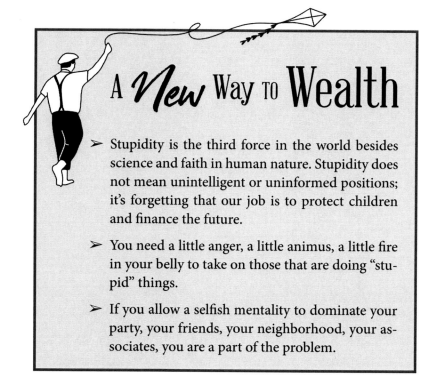

A *New* Way To Wealth

➤ Stupidity is the third force in the world besides science and faith in human nature. Stupidity does not mean unintelligent or uninformed positions; it's forgetting that our job is to protect children and finance the future.

➤ You need a little anger, a little animus, a little fire in your belly to take on those that are doing "stupid" things.

➤ If you allow a selfish mentality to dominate your party, your friends, your neighborhood, your associates, you are a part of the problem.

CHAPTER 8

✎

IN A WORLD OF NINE BILLION SOULS: WHAT LIFE LOOKS LIKE AT THE END OF THIS CENTURY

"Nor trivial Loss, nor trivial Gain despise;
Molehills, if often heap'd, to Mountains rise:
Weigh every small Expence, and nothing waste,
Farthings long sav'd, amount to Pounds at last."

—Ben Franklin, "How to Get Riches"

• •

Born in 1955, I will likely not see first-hand most of the second half of this century. My daughter Colette this week is now 25 years old, a quarter century; and I will be very lucky to see her visit when she is 50 years old. That does not bother me, as history is my guide, and I am a person of faith. But I can feel the urgencies of these next 50 years, and the social needs of her generation's future today as I write.

Most adults with children, whether rich or poor, can visualize 25 years into the future. Most mindful people, when childless, can do the same. This is not rocket science, but cultural common sense. Now is the time to end the delusion and the waste. Develop good habits of social governance. In a world of nine billion souls, remember the basic mantra of each chapter to thrive.

In reading a United Nations series of reports on "fragile states"[42] (what we used to call "failed states"), I can feel what scarcity does to the rule of law, and why governments fail when they are powerless to feed the poor. By 2021, there are

---

42 https://fragilestatesindex.org/

already 22 such states out of the 194 in the world. What will that look like in 2050, or perhaps 2090, unless we live the life of doing more with less?

In reading about climate change, and the inevitable nature of coastal flooding by 2050 or 2070, I imagined that life in my fable, *2040*. I reflected at length on how love of family and friends become essential elements of sportive seriousness to keep grounds for hope in a time of coastal floods and frequent climate storms.

There is a passage in *2040*, written during the Covid-19 pandemic in 2020, where I sum up my feelings and hopes about the near future:

> We have little left for reason before a storm surge of the size of those swallowing Japan, Australia's lovely coast, and my Long Island. The tornado proved my first glimpse of the under-world. Tornadoes do not dance with nuance, as the pursuit of atonement does in classical civilization. Climate storms lack the substance of teacher and colleague. It is all destruction, with little reason or moral.
>
> With all these losers and falsities before me, I went again to the wisdom in my backyard. There are a few human achievements that withstand climate storms. My favorite are the oaks on my property. I call them the oaks of liberty. They are six feet wide at the base, an amazing feat for biomass. In a storm I can watch my Allium get uprooted and my fields of perennials destroyed, but the oaks stand tall, only shedding an occasion-al old dead limb."

Humans are imaginative. There are feelings of grief, dread, joy in survival, surprise in the above passages—that is why I presented it as a fable. Humans have the ability to convert grief into grace and action.

We have the ability to forestall error; we have the energy to imagine taking turns for the better; we have the will to reshape our destiny. Be a creative soul, frugal and generous. Think often of the longevity of creation found in Bob Dylan's 65 years of productivity. It is about the giving for him, with wit and impact, not the money. He is the dance man, the tambourine man, singing that old time religion of music and grace, however odd his behaviors with people. Dylan lives in his own world, which has become a part of our own. You can develop the same kind of fidelity in your song with force and grace, after some effort.

Think positive about our shared future.

THE OPTIMISM BIAS

Tali Sharot demonstrated for *Time* magazine (Special Edition, June 2021, during Covid-19) how research has shown that the human brain is hardwired "to think positively." You can read entire books on this topic by other neuroscientists, as I have, but I will use Sharot to be my Bob Dylan here and sum it up in a short emotive song.

The *Time* cover article is an excerpt from Sharot's forthcoming book, *The Optimism Bias*, an investigation into our brains' neural tilt towards the positive, and how this bias plays a major part in determining how we live our lives. Early in the excerpt, the author identifies some essential and recurrent facts across all cultures. For example, people hugely underestimate...

- their chances of getting divorced;

- losing their job;

- being diagnosed with cancer;

- and even overestimating their likely life span (sometimes by as much as 20 years).

The essay then demonstrates what I have known since I was ten years old: it pays to have a positive attitude. One pull quote from Sharot notes:

> **To make progress, we need to be able to imagine alternative realities—better ones—and we need to believe that we can achieve them.**

Modern cognitive sciences, neurosciences, and clinical psychology suggest, rather vividly, that humans of all races and all nations have evolved these traits for good purpose. It helps us survive and position ourselves for a better life.

That is why I suggest that fate favors frugality. Put another way, fate *respects* frugality. It is the most positive insight I can give you as a competitor.

This is not delusion. This is not metaphysics. This is not mystical religion. Instead, it is a basic cognitive function.

Sure, we have "down" people, and profound artistic cynics, that add caution to the world. That is all good for the S Frontier. But the larger point of this new science, and of this book, is that it pays for you to develop a positive attitude.

What I want to add to this substratum of cognitive science is the social agenda that "doing more with less is success." And Micah Shippee's team will display that principle in a series of immersive experiences[43] the rest of this decade.

---

43 See: https://readylearner.one/ready-learner-one/

After watching my books *Doing More With Less* and *World Inc* travel the world of users, I've come to three fundamental beliefs:

1. **The future is near.** People all over care about the future, as they are hardwired to care about it. The trick is to help them align their money, people, and rules around competitive frugality. That is the path of more certain success, in a world filled with brutality, violence, and wrong thinking.

2. **Fate is a personal construct.** There will be many things that happen to you well beyond your control. But the fact remains that with the mantra of "doing more with less is success" before each of you each day, you can make fateful decisions weekly and shape your personal life.

3. **In the end all wealth is social wealth.** As Ben Franklin demonstrated to us again and again, being civil, being generous, and being in an exchange with a range of people allows this new kind of wealth.

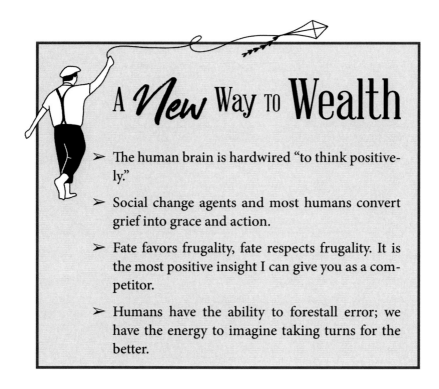

A *New* Way to Wealth

➤ The human brain is hardwired "to think positively."

➤ Social change agents and most humans convert grief into grace and action.

➤ Fate favors frugality, fate respects frugality. It is the most positive insight I can give you as a competitor.

➤ Humans have the ability to forestall error; we have the energy to imagine taking turns for the better.

*Temple of Olympian Zeus, Athens, begun in the 6th
century B.C. and completed in the 2nd century A.D.
during the reign of Emperor Hadrian.
Photo courtesy of Piasecki family.*

WE ARE WIRED FOR POSITIVE THINKING:
ONLY DOING MORE WITH LESS GETS US HOME

This book joins traditional American pragmatism, first articulated by Ben Franklin and William James, with global social needs.

You've now read chapters about megacities across the world, and their needs for heightened efficiencies. You have read about outsmarting knuckleheads, and reveled in the power and frugality of teams. I've asked you to think about Michael Jordan as an avatar of doing-more-with-less competitiveness.

This book points to the popular adoption of competitive frugality across more than 200 nations. It explains why corporations are being reshaped by capital markets, as demonstrated by the case of the brand-rich global firm Unilever. The middle chapters illustrated the logic and benefits that come from competing in a fair and open way in this new age marked by an emphasis on climate, environmental, and social and governance metrics. Now it's high time to sum up how all of this comes together.

In a world of many billions, this form of social response capitalism is both inevitable, and wanted. We will be the foster children of its family of products.

Yet we cannot implement solutions to these social problems without business leaders. This book places that point top and center.

I've already spoken about the pleasures I felt stepping up each rung on the ladder out of poverty. Pat Mahoney felt the same in making his life rich, saying in the earlier chapters: "I only regret that my children start too high with too much on the great chain of modern life." Pat thought it best for them to experience poverty, scarcity, and the will to inventiveness before running complex teams. But I think you can learn these principles yourself, and test them yourself, without first suffering.

Just a year prior to reading the above quote, I helped Pat Mahoney sell his surplus operating facility SEMASS, as part of closing a $1.2 billion facility deal. The week after the sale he told me, "Now I can start anew with creativity and return to the pleasures of being frugal." He did this many times in his life. Was he being foolish like a King Lear? "Not at all," he said.

"I can enter scenes of luxury when I want to lavish rewards on my family and friends, but I do not feel at home there." He wanted to return to the primal lens we explore in this book, a lens that helps you see through debt, confusion, and excess.

You can apply the same principles in running a bank, a manufacturing site, a global firm, or an investment company. You can see this in the "Less Is More" exhibit that now follows from Jack Robinson, one of the exemplar lives I wrote about in the book *Giants of Social Investing* (one of a series of business biographies). When I first met him, Jack was a banker, investor, and the Vice Chairman of the investment house Trillium. Listen to his advice to the new generation.

LESS IS MORE

By Jack Robinson
(investment house living legend)

My parents, Ed and Carolyn Robinson, wrote their bestselling book *The "Have-More" Plan* during WWII, a period marked by pervasive scarcity. The war not only took a serious toll on our country (in terms of both deaths and casualties), but it led to a dearth of life-sustaining necessities. Fueling the war machine became the nation's #1 priority, rendering commonplace gasoline lines, food shortages and geographical shortfalls in water supplies. As such, rationing became a way of life and simultaneously drove Americans to seek more of most everything because there simply were not adequate supplies of some of life's necessities.

The summer of 1945 marked the end of the war and came to signify the beginning of a pattern that we continue to experience today: an ever-accelerating demand for goods and services that exceeds our ability to utilize them efficiently or fully. With our now seemingly bountiful supply of most everything, our utilization rates are surprisingly low, and waste and inefficiency remain widespread throughout the system. In fact, we waste as much or more than half of the energy, food, and water produced in the U.S. each year. In a 2017 research report reprinted in the December 18, 2017 issue of *Fortune Magazine*, Dr. Joshua Rhodes and Dr. Michael Webber state unequivocally that "we waste about two-thirds of the roughly 100 quads (a quadrillion BTUs) of energy we consume each year." They go on to say that most of this waste results from the inefficient burning of fuels.

The "less is more" energy solution lies, in part, in the electrification of the economy, thereby improving energy efficiency. More electrons will be produced with less waste and pollution and at lower costs, especially for renewables-based power. For example, as buildings undergo decarbonization (e.g., converting heating systems to electric heat pumps), and electric vehicles (EVs) for transportation become more of the norm, the less efficient carbon fuel-based energy systems will be replaced with significant new efficiencies that will reduce costs, pollution, and waste.

Food represents another realm, or piece of the environmental puzzle, that has culminated in significant levels of waste. Food waste in America today is deplorable. In contrast with the food rationing during WWII, today 30–40% of our food supply is simply wasted, according to the U.S. Department of Agriculture (USDA). In turn, the many inputs to the wasted food supply chain such as water, energy, labor, and land are also squandered. Food loss occurs throughout the food supply chain—planting, growing, harvesting, transporting, storage, processing, packaging—not to mention the damage and spoilage that ensues throughout these processes. As for the demand side of our food system, individual and institutional buyers inevitably over-order, whether intentionally or by mistake. The result? Food waste at every step of the food supply-demand chain.

However, in an attempt to minimize such waste, in 2015 the United States Departments of Agriculture and Environmental Protection set a joint goal to reduce food waste in the country by 50% by the year 2030. While each agency introduced two very different measures to track results, the desired outcome of either or both would be a significant reduction in food waste. While there are many ways to reduce waste within the demand and supply spectrum for food, the two agencies agree that "the best approach to reducing food loss and waste is not to create it in the first place." In other words, less is more.

At last, this brings us to one of life's most vital ingredients: water. A significant target for environmental solutions, water lies at the very nexus of food and energy. While there were only occasional water shortages in the U.S. during WWII, the subsequent 75-year combination of climate change, population growth, development, and continuing wasteful water-use practices are leading to alarming water shortfalls in some parts of the country.

In August of 2021, the U.S. government declared that the Colorado River is in a "state of water shortage." As the river supplies water to six states and 40 million people, plus a $5 billion agriculture industry, that shortfall poses a serious challenge for the West and the entire country. According to a *Science News* article on September 25, 2001, titled "Rice in Trouble," low water levels in reservoirs and rivers in California have forced some farmers "to slash their water use by as much as 50%." Indeed, some California farmers have received no water this season.

Here again we have a real-time example of where less can and will be more. As the *Science News* article points out, 70% of the water used in flood irrigation for agriculture is wasted. Given that adequate water supplies simply do not exist, the agriculture industry will be forced to apply less intensive water practices such as drip irrigation. Drip irrigation can reduce water usage by more than 50% plus have the added benefit of reducing the unnecessary runoff of expensive crop enhancements.

Whether it be energy, food, or water, the country and, in fact, the world are in the process of recalibrating to a "less is more" mindset. Not only will we all waste less, we will become much more efficient in the resources that we enjoy.

If my parents were alive to rewrite their *"Have-More" Plan* today, surely it would be titled *Less Is More*.

Illustration Courtesy of: William Duke | Library of Congress

Big Ben—America's Big Ben, that is—went viral in a sense long before the internet, and has continued to do so ever since. While a smaller and smaller portion of capitalists remain lost in debt and speculative behaviors, the greater majority of the new generation want a response to climate change, and a lifestyle fashioned around competitive sustainability.

Ben Franklin taught me how to think, and I am sure he enabled the creation of the profit margins in my management consulting firm since 1981.

For this, many thanks.

THE WAY TO WEALTH

Benjamin Franklin's famous little essay, *The Way to Wealth*[44], is the witty reminder of how it pays to spend less, and gain more, both in gestures, attitude, and actual buying patterns.

Have you read it yet? It takes about an hour. Thinking about Ben again yesterday, I spent more than an hour aimlessly watering my many blooming flowers these excessively hot days in Saratoga. Yet Ben was near, I did not overwater. I did not waste their beauty. Better to care for them, Ben might say, than to waste them. It is being industrious while being frugal that matters most days.

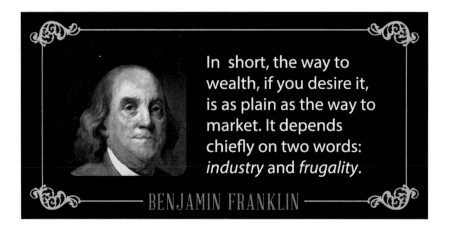

In short, the way to wealth, if you desire it, is as plain as the way to market. It depends chiefly on two words: *industry* and *frugality*.

— BENJAMIN FRANKLIN —

---

44 Full text of Franklin's *The Way to Wealth* is available online at Project Gutenberg: https://www.gutenberg.org/files/43855/43855-h/43855-h.htm

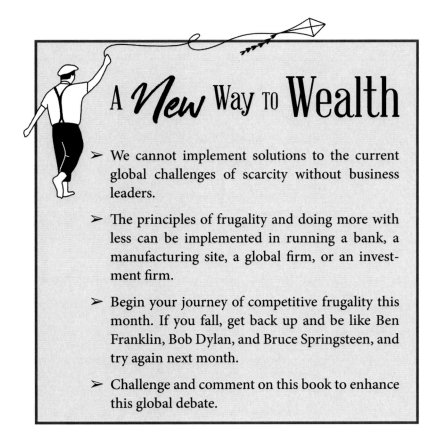

A *New* Way to Wealth

➤ We cannot implement solutions to the current global challenges of scarcity without business leaders.

➤ The principles of frugality and doing more with less can be implemented in running a bank, a manufacturing site, a global firm, or an investment firm.

➤ Begin your journey of competitive frugality this month. If you fall, get back up and be like Ben Franklin, Bob Dylan, and Bruce Springsteen, and try again next month.

➤ Challenge and comment on this book to enhance this global debate.

Appendix

Additional Reading

Below are listed a few key keepers for your shelves— classic titles that will stimulate your drive for a new way to wealth.

Lincoln on Leadership: Executive Strategies for Tough Times
By Donald T. Phillips

- Phillips dissects Lincoln under a microscope lens he's never been under before, connecting his incredible ability to unite and make decisions as a president to our economy as it operates in this moment.

- Lincoln's personality of immersion and deep contemplation allowed him to succeed as a war-time president, and can be brought forward to today in a business sense.

- The book helps us make ourselves, our family, and our firms more competitive by being financially prudent. It helps individual competitors become decisive. It helps your firm remain cost-effective. It helps society see your value as evidence-based and market-informed.

The Way to Wealth
By Benjamin Franklin

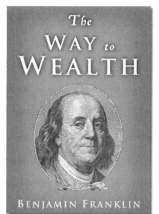

- Franklin's essay and its brilliant wit and adages are as relevant today as they were in 1758. Franklin provides advice on work ethic and frugality in economic terms as well as in life. "If you were a servant, would you not be ashamed that a good master should catch you idle? Are you then your own master? Be ashamed to catch yourself idle, when there is so much to be done for yourself, your family, your country."

Meditations
By Marcus Aurelius

- A series of notes and journal entries, *Meditations* is the great Roman emperor's thoughts on how to influence your perception of life through Stoicism, the practice of behaving virtuously despite the conditions outside your personal control, and by viewing these conditions rationally.

Good Business: The Talk, Fight, Win
Way to Change the World
By Bill Novelli

- *Good Business* inspires one to make choices, whatever they are, that create more while doing less. Novelli presents practical examples of how to perform meaningful work by getting everyone at the table, and telling, selling, and living your story.

- Novelli showcases his story from the beginning of his career as a humble soap salesperson after graduating from the University of Pennsylvania, through creation of his public relations firm Porter Novelli, which is now a member of the Omnicom Group, his founding of the Campaign for Tobacco-Free Kids, and his role as CEO of AARP, as an example of how to make social impact in a tactful and uncomplicated way.

- Novelli provides in-depth analysis of his process of talking and fighting to win against big tobacco, in concert with setting permanent values and principles built upon priceless and consistent communication.

Primed to Perform: How to Build the Highest Performing Cultures Through the Science of Total Motivation
By Neel Doshi and Lindsay McGregor

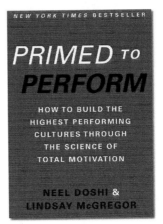

- Doshi and McGregor's *Primed to Perform* is a great compilation of cutting-edge psychological insights that can contribute to fostering a healthy and high-performing workplace culture.

- The book digs into the roots of a workplace culture's "magic" and reveals the layers of science that drive its performance in Parts I and II and provides insights and a step-by-step guide into how you can build a great culture that maximizes their principle of Total Motivation (or "ToMo") in Parts III and IV.

Start With Why: How Great Leaders Inspire Everyone to Take Action
By Simon Sinek

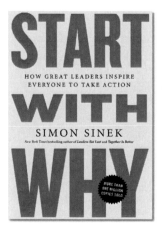

- Sinek's book is a must for any manager or entrepreneurial mind looking to lead and inspire by using his method of "starting with why." This method, Sinek explains, will outlast competitors who only think about the what or the how of their business.

- Starting with the why of a business may be difficult, but that's the challenge of creating a lasting business. Sinek shows how to lead those behind your cause to victory.

Michael Jordan and the New Global Capitalism
By Walter LaFeber

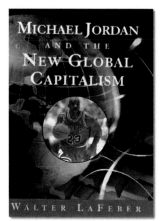

- Michael Jordan, the King of Competition, was a leading force in embracing a global retail and entertainment marketplace. LaFeber's biography and analysis is an incredible dive into both the tenacity of Jordan's competitive drive and ability, and the new era of global capitalism.

Competition Demystified: A
Radically Simplified Approach to
Business Strategy
By Bruce C. Greenwald
and Judd Kahn

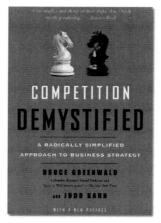

- Greenwald and Kahn's analysis
  of corporate strategy is fiercely simple in its method and
  strikingly effective. *Compe-*
  tition Demystified focuses on
  operational efficiency, and the
  question: "Are there barriers to
  entry that allow us to do things
  other firms cannot?"

ANNOUNCING
The Bruce Piasecki and Andrea Masters
$5,000 Annual Award on Business and Society Writing

Annual Deadlines: August 15, 2022 through 2045

Applicants must be between 18 and 40 years old and have at least one publication prior to that year's August 15 deadline date. These works can include essays, research papers, books, and articles. Topics must be thematically consistent with positive social impact and business. Themes include, but are not limited to, climate change, racial/gender equality, sustainability, and innovation.

To apply, send your published pieces (link or PDF) and a brief (1- to 2-page) working plan addressing your future writing endeavors and career to awards@ahcgroup.com (cc: debbi@ahcgroup.com).

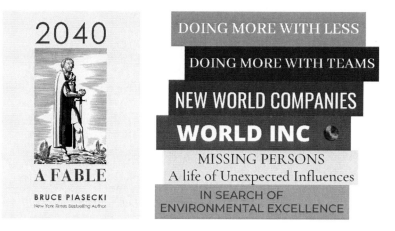

Creative Force Foundation, Inc was established to promote and support the literary arts and advance public appreciation of the same in order to educate the public on and raise awareness of sustainability issues that exist in the intersection between business and society.

This award is financed by Bruce Piasecki and the Creative Force Foundation, Inc.
www.DoingMoreWithLessBook.com

FULBRIGHT RECIPIENT DANIEL SHERRELL WINS

THE BRUCE PIASECKI AND ANDREA MASTERS ANNUAL AWARD ON BUSINESS AND SOCIETY WRITING FOR 2021

Daniel Sherrell

As announced by Square One Publishers on behalf of their author, Bruce Piasecki, Ph.D.[1]—the globally-minded sustainable environment trailblazer and bestselling business author of *Doing More With Less* and *New World Companies*, among others—has bestowed the 2021 Bruce Piasecki and Andrea Masters Annual Award on Business and Society Writing[2] upon Brown University Environmental Studies graduate and Fulbright grant recipient Daniel Sherrell.

---

1   https://www.ahcgroup.com/about-the-ahc-group/officers-and-staff-ahc-group/bruce-piasecki/

2   https://www.ahcgroup.com/about-the-ahc-group/creative-force-fund-annual-writing-award/2021-award-winner-daniel-sherrell/

Mr. Sherrell's award-winning essay, with its strong focus on climate change and his continuing role as Campaign Director for the Climate Jobs National Resource Center,[3] can be read at ahcgroup.com.[4]

Daniel Sherrell's first book, *Warmth: Coming of Age at the End of Our World*, was published in August 2021 and is available now.

To learn more about this story and to reach Dr. Piasecki, feel free to contact his office by email at:
awards@ahcgroup.com

---

3   https://www.cjnrc.org/

4   https://www.ahcgroup.com/mc_images/category/312/daniel-sherrell_2021-nys-writers-institute-award-statement.pdf

ANNOUNCING

An Immersive Experience on the Principles in Bruce Piasecki's books:

A joint venture with

With excitement and anticipation, I share news of this joint venture—our team's first virtual experience with you. *Doing More With Less* has been transformed into a four-part self-paced virtual course[1] (link goes to module 1 of 4) through a partnership with Ready Learner One that will help learners be able to:

1. Explore their roles as a leader in our changing society.

2. Enable themselves to navigate times when intervention is required to empower solutions from within their organization.

3. Leverage their leadership skills to use social capital to create a culture of frugality during tough economic times.

Upon completion of the course, the learner will be rewarded with a *Doing More With Less* Certification that can be shared with colleagues on their resumes and online profiles.

When my book *Doing More With Less* was first published, it became a *Washington Post Book World* and *New York Times* bestselling book. Touching on what works in the creative lives of Ben Franklin, Bob Dylan, and Bruce Springsteen, paperback editions

---

1   https://readylearner.one/ready-learner-one/

were recognized by *USA Today* and the *Wall Street Journal* on their bestseller top-ten lists. This is both lucky and rare, something we wish to share with you, your firm, and family.

You may ask: Why this reception across the decade?

My book takes a deep dive into our primal competitive instincts, as it embraces the idea of frugality, innovative self-actualization, and team loyalty as a crucial mix for a new world's competitive edge. It also made some fun of corporate and sports knuckle-heads along the way.

Over time, the principles behind this book became a powerful resource for a series of global organizations. From Toyota to Merck and Walgreens Alliance Boots, they turned the power of these competitive principles to help guide them to be leaders. In response, we are happy to release a new nine chapter book, *A New Way to Wealth: The Power of Doing More with Less*.

There is business value in strategic partnerships, as this new title comes along this Fall with this Ready Learner One certificate program for a new generation of users.

Why This Updated Immersive Experience First?

We live in a swift and severe world. Best to start now.

In today's fast-moving world, learners are seeking new ways to consume new information that is more engaging and allows them to learn when they want and at their own pace. Consequently, I have partnered with the company Ready Learner One[2] to transform my time-tested principles into a self-paced virtual course that will let any learner and corporate leader—across the globe before their computers or handhelds—become certified.

The great Benjamin Franklin once wrote:

> *The way to wealth is as plain as the way to market. It depends chiefly on two words, industry and frugality: that is, waste neither time nor money, but make the best use of both. Without industry and frugality nothing will do, and with them everything.*

My course launched on October 8, 2021, as an add-on during the Ready Learner One Innovations Beta Lab, a virtual learning opportunity that will bring learner–leaders from companies such as Nike, Amazon, and HP together with our clients and readers. Bring these masterful firms and my principles into your organization through this joint venture.

Register for Ready Learner One's Innovations Beta Lab[3] so you can learn from other global leaders. You may wish to start by enrolling in this self-paced training from my books[4] through their platform. Swiftly, you can become certified on your further path to success.

---

2   https://readylearner.one/

3   https://readylearner.one/events/

4   https://readylearner.one/ready-learner-one/

Dr. Bruce Piasecki is the founder of a global management consulting firm, AHC Group, Inc. (www.ahcgroup.com). You can learn more about Piasecki's life through his memoir, *Missing Persons*. With his wife Andrea Carol Masters and his daughter and others, Bruce established the Creative Force Foundation, Inc. Its purpose is to provide global annual awards to young writers on Business and Society issues like climate change.